Tim Rappleye's latest book confirms Baker's status as a true legend: an incredible athlete, hockey's first American star — the Bobby Orr of his era – who was idolized by F. Scott Fitzgerald while at Princeton. Rappleye's original research, including letters from confidants and eye-witnesses, convincingly solves the century-old mystery of Baker's death at the close of World War I. If you like hockey, history, or a good story, you'll like *Hobey Baker: Upon Further Review.*

—JOHN U. BACON, AUTHOR OF THE NATIONAL BESTSELLER *THE GREAT HALIFAX EXPLOSION*

As a college hockey fanatic and a Princeton alum, I felt well versed in the Hobey story, but Tim Rappleye's book introduced me to many more layers of the legend. His research and storytelling live up to Hobey's exemplary standard.

—NATE EWELL, COLLEGE HOCKEY, INC.

Hobey Baker is known as the hockey legend from Princeton and St. Paul's School. Leave it to Tim Rappleye to discover that Baker is an original Philadelphia hockey guy, a player who lost a tooth de-fending his brother in a South Philly shinny scrap. Rappleye's telling of Hobey's farewell to hockey has created a whole new chapter in American hockey history. If you care about hockey, *Hobey Baker, Upon Further Review* belongs on your shelf.

—KEITH JONES, NHL ON NBC

PRAISE FOR *JACK PARKER'S WISEGUYS*

A terrific read for fans and players familiar with that rough-and-tumble hockey vintage.

—BOBBY ORR

A must-read book about a Division I dynasty and its Hall of Fame coach.

—LOU LAMORIELLO, STANLEY CUP-WINNING GM

HOBEY BAKER

UPON FURTHER REVIEW

EXPLORING THE LIFE AND DEATH
OF A HOCKEY IMMORTAL

TIM RAPPLEYE

MISSION POINT PRESS

Readers are encouraged to go to www.MissionPointPress.com
to contact the author or to find information on how to buy this
book in bulk at a discounted rate.

Published by Mission Point Press
2554 Chandler Rd.
Traverse City, MI 49686
(231) 421-9513
www.MissionPointPress.com

Cover and interior design by Heather Lee Shaw

ISBN: 978-1-943995-73-8
Library of Congress Control Number: 2018945926

Printed in the United States of America.

To my brother Charles, kingpin of the Rappleye journos.

Contents

Hobey Baker's image still resides in Princeton's Ivy Club foyer.
(Tim Rappleye)

Introduction

Hobey Baker's Death is the startling end note of a 20th century fairy tale that defies belief. America's most beautiful sportsman dying in the arms of his Princeton professor with his orders home from The Great War tucked in his leather flying jacket is hopelessly romantic. His fall from the sky was the farewell splash of Icarus, a Chip Hilton installment with a cruel twist, the conclusion of a tragic Fitzgerald novel.

Hobey Baker's resume—the last man to die in World War I and the first man inducted into Hockey's Hall of Fame—barely scratches the surface of the emotional impact Baker had on everyone he touched in his 27 years on earth, and those who were smitten by his legend years later.

It is no coincidence that Princeton contemporary F. Scott Fitzgerald featured several versions of Hobey in his novels. Not only was he the heroic football captain of Fitzgerald's college life, but Baker spent several years as the poster-child for male beauty and grace amidst the wealthy Long Island aristocracy that was later portrayed in *The Great Gatsby*.

Readers might recall the January 2018 news flash when a cache of letters from a World War I fighter pilot was discovered, and then put up for auction. Lieutenant Edgar Taylor's letters were valued at over $10,000. They contained action highlights quite similar to Hobey's from his days as a World War I pursuit pilot, with the same jargon and the cool demeanor befitting the glamorous knights of the sky. Hobey's letters from the Great War are far more extensive than Taylor's, and just as dramatic. Captain Baker was a U.S. Army pursuit pilot as skilled as any in the romantic Lafayette Escadrille, and his deadly encounters with Baron von Richtofen's *Flying Circus* are described here in gripping detail.

It was not war heroics that made Hobey a household name, however, but the glory he achieved on the playing fields of Princeton. Hockey and football at the turn of the century were often considered blood sport by the Pulitzer and Hearst broadsheets that chronicled them. But then came the beautiful Baker, with his unmistakable blonde mane unencumbered by a helmet, taming these barbarians with his raw speed and feline instincts. College Football was the country's most popular amateur sport in the early 20th century, and despite being the lightest man on the field, Hobey played his way into the Hall of Fame.

But it was hockey that elevated Hobey to sports immortality. His mind-blowing performances up in Canada forever changed our neighbors' perception of American Hockey, prompting Toronto's Hockey Hall of Fame to usher him into their exclusive club at first opportunity. Baker's gentlemanly play, not only his scoring prowess, colored every description of him.

December 2018 marks the centennial of Hobey's tragic death, but his name continues to generate headlines. The *Hobey Baker Award* commemorates college hockey's player of the year; it is awarded annually for more than just performance; it honors sportsmanship as well, a trait many feel is long forgotten today.

Baker's seemingly gilded life was followed by his premature death—testing a flawed plane on a final flight—which has made him one of the most romantic sports figures in American lore. *Sports Illustrated* published a magnificent story on Hobey in 1991, prompting ESPN to rewrite most of its opening fanfare for that year's NCAA hockey championship telecast as a tribute to Baker's legend. Analyst Barry Melrose frequently swoons over Hobey during his on-air commentary. Everyone who attends the annual Hobey Baker Award presentation all mourn the hero who died far too young. It's as if Hobey returns to visit his hockey legions each spring.

But Baker's history is far more complex than the polished version presented every year by the Hobey Baker Award Committee. There is compelling evidence, and much speculation, that Hobey's death was not an accident. His life growing up was no fairy tale: parental scandal, a mother's abandonment, and the loss of family fortune. He met a *femme fatale* in World War I France and was never able to break her spell. He had an elder male admirer with whom he roomed for two years after college, igniting a disconcerting whisper campaign. Hobey masked a slew of dark secrets up until that fateful moment, 350 feet above earth, when he made the ill-fated decision to turn back to his airfield with a dead engine.

This work examines Baker with a sober lens, bolstered by hundreds of letters, freshly surfaced newspaper stories, a trove of new interviews, and a gripping eyewitness account of Baker's last day alive. Readers will also find micro-chapters calked *Hobeyquests*, the author's forays into the field to try and flesh out modern connections to our century-old protagonist.

Based on the merger of all this new information with old, in a 21st century prism, the reader can finally make sense of the hundred-year-old mystery of Hobey's death. Hobart Amory Hare Baker is no longer a sepia-stained image in a dusty frame; he is flesh and blood, with the same foibles, fears and dreams that the rest of us face daily. One hundred years in the making, the legend finally appears in a critical light: *Hobey Baker, Upon Further Review.*

Hobey Baker, Toul, France, 1918. (Princeton University)

Prologue
Toul

Heff Herring woke with a start. He was roused by what sounded like an explosion just outside his window. He cracked open a bloodshot eye and spied the clock on his night stand—two minutes before 5:00 a.m. The munitions office strained his neck and peaked outdoors. It was the shortest day of the year, so the only light came from the quarter moon. He thought he saw two men aboard a combination motorcycle exiting the gate, heading north. Herring noticed it was raining. He cursed and rolled over.

Six hours later Herring stoked the coals at the center of the officers' quarters; chestnuts were roasting on the stove. The Toul aerodrome was now a dead zone: five weeks after the World War I Armistice, the only activity was from the handful of officers stirring Benedictine into their cognac. Nearly 400 members of the U.S. Army were stationed at this outpost in northeast France, all simply biding their time, waiting for their orders home. All but one, thought Herring.

Captain Hobey Baker had confided in Herring the day before about his orders home, sharing his misgivings about abandoning his troops. Herring, Baker's former professor and football coach at Princeton, urged Hobey not to go to Paris to appeal his orders, which is precisely what he had done, ignoring his former mentor's advice in the pre-dawn hours.

Another mini-explosion in the late morning shook a dozen officers from their malaise. The two-seated motorcycle had returned to the airfield, backfiring during a downshift as it bounced through the east gates. The men balanced their drinks and peeked through the shutters, a smile coming to their faces. The commanding officer of the 141st Aero Squadron, Hobey Baker, was now straddling the engine of the bike, his designated driver Howard Nieland in the side car—feet up and chomping a fat cigar. Baker brought their vehicle to a sudden stop right at the door to the officer's quarters, the engine belching smoke as he hopped into the cozy room.

Herring sat back and watched Captain Baker parade through the room with manic energy, teasing his fellow officers by waiving his orders home under their noses. As expected, Colonel Lahm had dismissed Hobey's appeal to delay his departure as soon as he heard the request in Paris. Baker was now back with his troops, engaging them in this flippant farewell. Herring was the only one not amused; he had known Baker longer than anyone in the room and he'd never seen his protégé so irreverent. The day's events began to unfold at a speed and manner that Herring not only disapproved of, but was powerless to control.

"I'm going to take the old Spad for one last flight," said Baker, which caused at least one man to choke on his cognac. Herring's immediate protest was echoed by the other men. Superstition was a way of life in the Army Air Corps, and everybody in that wooden shack knew the drill: pilots had but a two-week life expectancy in their wicker and wire contraptions. No one in their right mind would test the fates in a meaningless flight.

Herring knew his commanding officer wasn't kidding about getting airborne once again; at his core Hobey was a thrill-seeker, and now he was looking for one last adrenaline high. Herring pushed to the front of the pack and got into Hobey's face, imploring him to reconsider. Baker waved him away and marched outside toward the hangar, looking for his trusty aircraft, Spad Number 2.

The hangar was unusually quiet; planes scattered around the perimeter like mannequins. Baker was greeted by one of the few humans in the shop, the squadron's chief mechanic. "Captain Baker, sir, Number 7 is ready for a flight test." As soon as he heard the mechanic utter those words, Herring felt an emotion he had not experienced since being transferred to Toul a month earlier—terror. His best friend in the squadron was about to take a foolhardy flight in an untested craft, a plane whose carburetor had failed its last time out. Herring finally caught up to Hobey in mid-stride, grabbed him by the shoulders, and forced a compromise.

"Promise me you will fly straight out to Pont-a-Mousson and back, and land without acrobatics," said Herring, who was fighting back emotions, his day turning into a nightmare. Baker made eye contact, nodded, and hopped the wing to climb into the cockpit.

HOBEY BAKER: UPON FURTHER REVIEW

Wissahickon Creek, Philadelphia. A two-minute walk from Baker's first home, the Creek was one of the city's most popular ice skating venues. (Lower Merion Historical Society)

CHAPTER 1

Scandal!

Hobart Amory Hare Baker was born into Philadelphia society on January 15, 1892.[1] Jefferson University Hospital president Dr. Hobart Amory Hare, his Aunt Rebecca's husband, presided over his birth. Hobey's home for the first eight years of his life was on 104 Rochelle Road in the Wissahickon neighborhood of Philadelphia, a modest house nestled between the Schuylkill River and Wissahickon Creek. The creek abutted the land behind Baker's back yard, and being much shallower than the river, it would freeze for weeks longer during the winter. Three months a year, Hobey and his brother Thornton (a year older) would hike 500 feet through the woods with hockey sticks and blades, enjoying a competitive skate whenever they felt the urge.

The Pemberton sisters—Hobey's mom Mary and Rebecca Hare—often merged their families. The Bakers and the Hares shared European vacations together, a frequent subject of the Philadelphia society pages. When they were back in the city, the Hares often helped raise the two Baker boys.

Hobey's father was Alfred "Bobby" Baker, a successful entrepreneur in the upholstery business and a former halfback for the Princeton Tigers. The son of one of Philadelphia's prominent Episcopal ministers, Baker belonged to the most exclusive WASP clubs in Philadelphia. Hobey's mother, Mary Pemberton

Baker, had a storied heritage as well, including a great uncle who was a civil war hero. She was described by a relative as a "strong looking, rather handsome woman with classic Grecian features, blonde hair and a high color." [2] Mary's fiery independence made her an outlier from the Episcopal society women of the early 20th century.

The Baker marriage was colored by discord. By the time the family and four servants moved across the Schuylkill River in 1900 to a mansion in Bala Cynwyd, the two parents were in a state of "mutual dereliction," according to biographer John Davies. [3] Mom's unbridled spirit was difficult to accept in the Puritanical enclaves of Philadelphia society, particularly when it manifested itself in affairs of the heart. "The beautiful but frivolous former Mary Pemberton," reported the New York City tabloids, "managed to keep the Quaker City gossips in turmoil for many years before she and Alfred were finally separated for all times." [4] One can only imagine Bobby Baker's anger and humiliation upon hearing the whispers of his wife's dalliances while making the rounds at the Racquet Club, the Rittenhouse Club and Philadelphia's most exclusive club, the Fish House. Meanwhile, his own indiscretions, while having a permanent impact on his life and health, were not nearly as scandalous as those of his wife.

The two boys were frequently shuttled between prep schools as their parents' marriage unraveled at the turn of the century. In September of 1900, Hobey and Thornton entered Episcopal Academy in Philadelphia, known widely as the city's finest private day school. When they weren't in class, they were often farmed out to Rebecca and Dr. Hare's residence downtown. Although Hobey was losing touch with his biological mom, he received ample maternal love from both Aunt Rebecca and his cousin Mary, the latter eight years his elder. A gifted wordsmith,

Mary Amory Hare always held a special place in her heart for cousin Hobey.

With mom reportedly in Europe from July through September in 1902, Hobey and Thornton were pulled from Episcopal Academy and sent to boarding school 80 miles west of Philadelphia. The Yeates School in Lancaster was America's most expensive prep school. Before the boys completed the 1902-03 school year, they learned that their parents had separated and were preparing to divorce, unleashing a feeding frenzy in the Philadelphia society pages.

Divorce was an unimaginable scandal in Protestant Philadelphia at the time, so in September of 1903 Bobby Baker took pre-emptive action. He jettisoned the boys 350 miles north to the Saint Paul's School (SPS), far away from Eastern Pennsylvania and its echo chambers of toxic family rumors. Bobby's cousin James Conover was a longtime master at St. Paul's, an Episcopal educational enclave deep in the woods of Concord, New Hampshire. At the time, Hobey was 11 years old, Thornton 12. It was their third prep school in three years, but it would be their last. The boys spent the rest of their childhood being raised by Protestant masters in the patriarchal barracks of St. Paul's.

Ned Toland, an SPS senior (Form VI) at the time, recalled being approached by Hobey's father when he dropped off his youngest in Concord. "We can't do much about bringing up this boy," said the elder Baker to Toland. "Please keep an eye on him." [5] Both Hobey and Thornton were entering Form I, the equivalent of seventh grade. At 11 years old, Hobey was nearly a full year younger than his classmates. Having big brother Thornton at his side provided critical support during yet another adjustment period.

Mary and Alfred Baker finalized their divorce in the Philadelphia courts in 1905, two years into the boys' tenure at St.

Paul's. There is no record of Hobey ever having meaningful contact with his mother again. Princeton's Hobey Baker archives do not contain a single reference to Hobey's mother until 1917, when she was mentioned in a letter to Hobey while he was serving in World War I.

Hobey's childhood friend Elizabeth Roberts, a prominent member of Philadelphia society herself, shared the prevailing sentiments of 1900's WASP aristocracy towards Mary Baker: "Hobey's mom would have been called a mental case because she was so into men," wrote Roberts. [6] At the turn of the 20th century, promiscuous women were frequently diagnosed with "hysteria" simply for possessing a sex drive. Offenders were often committed to psych wards, full of male doctors eager to employ draconian surgery.

There are several reports of Mary Pemberton Baker being institutionalized for her transgressions, though no actual documents have surfaced. The understanding within the St. Paul's hockey community is that Hobey's mom was in an asylum while he was at school. "Very strange, the whole thing," said Parker Packard, a Saint Paul's hockey player from the class of 1955. "She, in fact, was committed to an asylum, and he [Hobey] was not allowed to see her even when he would go home on vacations. The doctor said it will not help him, it will not help her." [7]

According to the *Philadelphia Enquirer*, in July of 1905 Mary Baker was living at the Van Rensselaer apartment hotel in Manhattan at the time of their messy public divorce, commuting to Philadelphia for the court hearings. The article said that "after the settlement of the case she intends to sail for Europe for an indefinite stay." [8] And *poof!* Mary Pemberton vanished, her trail running ice cold for a dozen years.

As a woman of means in the early 20th century, facing a potential commitment to an asylum, Mary Baker would have been wise to get the hell out of Dodge. What we do know is that when Hobey's mom resurfaced in 1917 she has remarried. At some point during her dark period Mary Pemberton wed New York native Frederick Van Shutts, a wedding that escaped the eye of American newspapers. Regardless of how she spent the years from 1905 to 1917, she was missing from Hobey's life, and her absence cannot be underestimated in terms of its impact on his psychological and emotional development.

St. Paul's Lower School Pond, the wintertime assembly line that produced America's premier hockey talent for over half a century. (St. Paul's School)

CHAPTER TWO

Seven Years in the Cradle

For aristocrats in the early 20th century, St. Paul's boarding school in Concord, New Hampshire was the best place to foster the next generation of American leaders. Hobey's second cousin J.P. Conover remembers when the Baker boys first set foot on campus. "Hobart and Thornton were entirely unknown to me until their father brought them up to St. Paul's. Two sturdy little boys in trousers and Eton collars, Hobart with very light hair, almost tow-headed." [1] Although Thornton was 12 and Hobey 11, they both entered Form I of St. Paul's, the equivalent of today's 7th grade. Hobey was the youngest of the 320 boys enrolled that year, but he did have the security of a loving sibling within shouting distance at all times.

Hobey and Thornton were now ensconced in the patriarchal world of St. Paul's. Their days were spent surrounded entirely by men: proctors, masters, upperclassmen and classmates. They all dutifully marched to the Episcopalian beat that would propel most of the boys into elite Ivy League schools, and ultimately into the halls of American power. It was a world of conformity: buttoned up collars, daily prayer, and classwork that required dedicated repetition. Every afternoon, however, the boys were rewarded with massive helpings of team sports. The two brothers from Philadelphia, athletes by nature with no home life to return to, embraced it all.

There is no record that Bobby Baker had any inkling that his cousin James Conover was a hockey missionary, but turning over young Hobey to this St. Paul's master was the ideal formula to create a hockey prodigy, the likes of which had never been seen. A decade before Hobey was born, the ever-curious Conover went to hockey's epicenter of Montreal to learn all he could about the fledgling sport. After scouting dozens of games, he returned to St. Paul's with sticks, a rulebook, and an octagonal wooden puck covered in leather, one that could actually slide across the ice. That trip was the catalyst of Saint Paul's rise to prominence, and eventually the school acquired its title as the "Cradle of American Hockey," a moniker earned from 60 years of eastern hockey domination.

Conover described his foray in a letter plucked from the SPS archives. "I got sticks, pucks and rules from Canada myself," wrote Conover. "We flooded the field just below the dam with a few inches of water so we had safe and early skating. So we put teams on the pond." [2] Hobey's coach was a Conover disciple named Malcolm Gordon, the most astute mind in prep hockey for several decades. He is credited with writing America's first hockey rulebook in 1884.

By the time Hobey arrived in 1903, Gordon had already turned SPS into a veritable hockey factory. When the temperatures plunged after Thanksgiving, boards were erected on Lower School Pond to create seven regulation rinks (200' x 85'), with two adjacent practice rinks. Horse drawn sleighs scraped and planed the ice to keep the operation humming well into March. The natural ice of St. Paul's was the assembly line that bred hockey stalwarts for the Ivy League's "Big Three"—Yale, Harvard, and Princeton—for over half a century.

St. Paul's students were broken up into internal athletic clubs very much like Hogwarts School of Harry Potter fame, but instead of *Gryffindor*, Hobey and Thornton represented *Isthmian*, who battled against *Old Hundred* and *Delphian* throughout the year in football, hockey and baseball. Hobey and Thornton competed side-by-side for six years for Isthmian. Each spring they rowed crew for the Shattuck Club, and together they participated in the annual "Hare and Hounds" foot race.

But make no mistake, it was hockey that pushed the pulse at St. Paul's: over 300 boys would play incessantly for four months on St. Paul's natural ice. Intramural contests were often played at a higher level than the occasional games against outsiders. St. Paul's selected the best of its club players to create the equivalent of an All-Star varsity, a squad that played, and frequently beat, Ivy League teams whose rosters were invariably stocked with St. Paul's grads. Hobey fielded punts in the fall, handled pitchers on the grassy diamond each spring, but it was on the black ice of SPS where his body flew and his spirits soared.

Imagine Hobey's arrival at a foreign campus as an 11-year-old child, a boy who had just been severed from his mom. Young Baker channeled all that confused emotion and energy into hockey, the activity that brought him the most attention at St. Paul's. It was a facsimile of love from the sports-mad community cloaked in red and white.

"If you don't have a mother, you want her approval," said Bruce Smith, 1960 Yale hockey captain and a man devoted to raising Hobey's legend from the dead. Smith has written two screenplays about Baker's life, and he sculpted a bronze image of Hobey that lives in the Hockey Hall of Fame. He is convinced that Hobey's intense work ethic, manifested on the ice up in Concord, came from the anguish of losing contact with his mother. "That love was certainly lacking in his life," said Smith. "I think that is one of the things that really hurt him, and drove him." [3]

Pete Bostwick, Jr. was a hockey star at St. Paul's in the early 1950's, and knew first-hand how the institution would cultivate its talent at first frost. SPS masters would occasionally drive their prodigies to Turkey Pond, a long shallow pond half a mile from campus, to get in the earliest skates possible. "There were three or four masters involved with hockey," said Bostwick, "and they would take the hockey players at six o'clock in the morning to special little ponds that were well protected or quite shallow, that froze a little bit quicker. It was a special treat to be invited by one of the masters to go and play some shinny on a pond at six o'clock in the morning before you went to school." [4]

Whether it was on Turkey Pond in November, or Lower School Pond in December, the first ice at St. Paul's was known as "black ice," the virginal track with no accumulation of snow to slow a flashing blade. The black ice of SPS had a reputation throughout eastern hockey as the fastest in the land. Teams visiting St. Paul's for games in December were known to have had their "doors blown off" by the unnerving speed of the hosts in cherry and white sweaters, flying down the black ice at a pace never before seen, let alone defended.

Hobey was clearly a chosen one, and he not only embraced the opportunity for extra ice-time at St. Paul's, but doubled down. In addition to the sanctioned dawn skates with masters, he stole away at night, going for midnight forays guided only by the stars, the moon and his innate balance. He brought out a stick and puck, and became a stickhandling wizard in the pitch black.

"That was a big contribution to his learning to skate," said his nephew Hobey Baker II, Thornton's son. "He could go out at night in the dark, that's how you learned to hold the puck on the stick so well, you couldn't see the end of the stick." [5]

Screenwriter Smith spent most of his early life immersed in hockey, but he had never encountered anyone with Hobey's intensity. "I haven't read about anybody as driven as he was, to make himself into a performer, an athlete," said Smith. "The way he went about it, Hobey out there skating alone at night, on that rink." [6]

Hobey was instantly possessed by the sport that was frozen religion at the northern New England outpost. The four-month seasons on Lower School Pond became Hobey's laboratory as he transformed himself into a master of the sport at a young age, and then pushed himself to another, never-before-seen level. He soon acquired the 10,000 hours author Malcolm Gladwell insists are required for "genius" status. His brilliance was impossible to ignore; as a 15-year-old, he was thrust into the prestigious role of SPS hockey captain in mid-season, a majestic title he would hold for an additional two years.

Hockey's timeless equation is that greatness is a product of ice time, and Hobey yearned for more. Former Yale captain John Schley, a product of St. Paul's from the 1950's, recalled a conversation he had with venerable master Howell "Patsy" Campbell at the SPS dining hall. Campbell was a St. Paul's hockey captain when Hobey was an underclassman, and helped Hobey steal more of those precious moments on ice. "He (Campbell) told me the story how on Sundays they were not allowed to play hockey," said Schley, "but they would go to the far end of the pond beyond the sight of any school buildings. They would hide their skates along the banks of the pond under the tree roots, go there on Sundays to pull the skates out which had buckles on them that they would easily fasten and unfasten, and escape the notice of any of the masters. Then he took me out and showed me where Hobey hid his skates, under the roots of a large tree." [7]

Hobey's passion for ice time extended to the spring, when he rowed crew for the Shattuck club. On their first voyages out on Turkey Pond each spring, Hobey was often distracted, spying the shallow and shaded shorelines, seeking out any remaining ice suitable for skating.

Hobey sought every edge that could accelerate his budding

genius, and he discovered a partner in veteran SPS equipment man Johnny Mack. Hobey allowed Mack to "rocker" his skates, grinding down the front and back ends of Hobey's blades into the shape of a rocking chair. This was a technical breakthrough, never before done in the United States. Before "rockering," early 20th century hockey skates resembled today's goalie skates— nine inches of steel lying flat on the ice like a ruler. At the turn of the previous century, Baker and Mack combined to create a breakthrough in sports science, the venerable craftsman tinkering with the prodigy's wings. Hobey's "rockered" blades allowed him to cut tight circles around opponents in his daring forays up and down the ice. Baker's signature move was to circle his own goal once, sometimes twice, before accelerating out of the last turn and screaming down the ice. None of that would be possible if not for the two men's combined creativity.

The rules of the day seemed tailored to Hobey's unique skill set. Prior to 1920, official hockey games were played with seven men per side, all the positions of today's game, *plus* a "rover." The three forwards would all skate their lanes like the table hockey games of one's childhood, except for the rover, who would go wherever his spirit dictated. Baker was born to play that position, flying around all four corners of the rink at top speed, if not with the puck, then in hot pursuit.

After dominating middle school hockey for three years, Hobey made the St. Paul's varsity at the tender age of 14. On his first varsity road trip, he travelled with the squad to New York City for its annual holiday festival, a chance to play other prep schools or St. Paul's alums in front of the SPS New York family. His first game away from campus was December 20, 1906, a 6-0 victory over St. Mark's. The St. Paul's publication *The Record* has the first documented write-up from a Hobey game: "Baker shined. He was at his best in New York and in the varsity game, where the smooth hard ice aided his quickness with the puck." [8] This was his first visit to Saint Nicholas Arena, the largest hockey venue in the eastern United States at the time, a block from Broadway on West 66th Street. Both the player and the audience were left with a profound impression.

After the game, Baker joined his teammates for some public skating alongside the regular patrons of Saint Nicholas Arena. Hobey was in awe of the great barn: an extra-large 200' by 90' ice sheet, framed by low hanging balconies that could hold 4,000 fans. Without intending to, Hobey's engine began to rev up. He started using the public skaters as virtual slalom poles, and began accelerating through his turns. Although he didn't make contact with anyone, the ladies and gentlemen enjoying a leisurely evening skate were startled by the blonde comet whizzing by. Before long, rink manager Bill Leonard had to whistle Hobey to the boards. "I had to go out and warn him to put on the brakes," said Leonard. [9] Hobey blushed red, apologized profusely, and resumed skating. Unable to contain his need for speed, however, Hobey once again tore through the crowd, as Leonard shook his head. After several more laps around the race track, Hobey was flagged down for the night. "It was no use," said Leonard. "He simply couldn't make his skates behave, and I finally had to order him off the ice for good." [10] Leonard had caught an early glimpse of what the rest of New York's sporting public would come to hold dear for the next decade, the *Hobey Rush*. Saint Nicholas Arena became Baker's hockey Mecca, the forerunner to Madison Square Garden. It was here that he became America's first hockey superstar.

Due to his early arrival and a post-graduate senior year, Hobey spent one year beyond the supposed maximum for a St. Paul's student. Over those seven years he was an eager disciple of Hall-of-Fame hockey master Malcolm Gordon. He spent four years as a star on the SPS varsity, leading them to frequent victories over Ivy League varsities. Due to a twist of fate (a common occurrence in Baker's mythological life), the country's most ravenous media circus discovered Hobey when he was a 16-year-old schoolboy.

In December of 1908, the Saint Paul's hockey squad took its regular pilgrimage to New York City, this time scheduled to play decided underdog Lawrenceville School. But an epidemic of scarlet fever forced the New Jersey preps to cancel at the last minute. The managers of Saint Nicholas Arena had already sold tickets and were in a tight spot. They asked their highly touted tenants, a collection of former college stars and transplanted Canadians known appropriately as St. Nick's, if they would help out the Ice House management by standing in for Lawrenceville. Keep in mind that St. Nick's was comprised of hardened men who had won regional championships and battled top Canadian amateur teams tooth and nail. In keeping with the holiday spirit, however, they agreed to help out their landlords and play the game, expecting to toy with the pups from up north. Since St. Nick's home games always included a bevy of New York sportswriters, press row was full that night, each newspaperman anticipating a lopsided mismatch. What they got instead was a 40-minute glimpse of a fantastical hockey future.

Baker and his prep mates wowed the fans and especially the cynical scribes. Although St. Paul's fell to St. Nick's by a 3-1 score, the papers claimed that St. Paul's had largely outplayed their elders, and in the closing minutes, "pandemonium" reigned in the stands. [11] It was the first time a sporting crowd had seen an individual so dominate the ice, as St. Paul's young captain Baker repeatedly rushed the puck end-to-end, bringing fans out of their seats and guttural roars from their lungs. According to SPS records, Hobey weighed a mere 148 pounds that season. [12] The fans and writers in attendance never forgot the willowy lad with the hardiest endurance on the frozen sheet that night. Despite having played at the Saint Nicholas Arena the previous two years, December 15, 1908 was Hobey's true "debut" on America's premier hockey venue.

Baby-boomers may recall Bobby Orr's impact in 1966 on the forlorn fans of the downtrodden Boston Bruins, as the 18-year-old sensation with the blonde buzz cut gave them fresh dreams of future glory. Imagine the response to a 16-year-old hockey phenom in the Big Apple. Fans in the hockey hotbeds of Boston, Toronto, Montreal and Ottawa would all eventually revel in the Hobey experience. They witnessed the blonde man-child playing high speed keep-away, often circling the same defenders repeatedly en route to the opposition goal, before burying the puck in the back of the net. Those electrifying rushes are what compelled Hockey's Hall of Fame in Toronto to welcome Baker into their exclusive club at first opportunity.

Hobey's seven-year reign at St. Paul's were his critical formative years. We know he was a hockey superstar, having rapidly accrued his 10,000 Gladwellian hours. But what occurred in the other components of Hobey's development? How well was this now-motherless boy developing into a man? The *Saint Paul's Record* kept meticulous notes on each athlete, so we have precise data as to Hobey's size: as a 16-year-old in the spring of 1908, Hobey was a shade over 5'7" and weighed 145 pounds; after that summer's vacation he reported to football an inch taller and three pounds heavier. The Record's final entry for Hobey was prior to the spring's crew season of 1910. The 18-year-old post-grad had filled out to within five pounds of his college playing size—a human panther at 5'9", 155 pounds. [13] In every athletic endeavor on the sports-mad campus of St. Paul's that year, Baker was a man amongst boys. His extra year, known as an "Upper Reserve," was not unique—boys often needed a year of seasoning before going on to college. Today it is known as a "Post-Graduate" or "P.G." year.

There are other metrics to track Hobey's growth: When

Hobey joined the SPS choir his first year he was a treble who performed cantoris; by year three he was an alto, and in his senior spring he was a bass in the glee club, performing "Soldiers' Farewell" and "Old St. Paul's." One can read into Hobey's character by his love of singing. There are recollections from Hobey's classmates of his reedy soprano solos flowing out from the morning chapel choir, singing "O for the Wings of a Dove."

> *Oh, for the wings, for the wings of a dove,*
> *Far away, far away would I rove!*
> *Oh, for the wings, for the wings of a dove,*
> *Far away, far away, far away, far away would I rove!* [14]

Hobey's mind was being trained as well, earning kudos for his debating skills. In the Cadmean - Concordian Literary Society joint debate, he was named best debater on the subject of "The History of Trade Unions for the past 20 Years Shows a Tendency Detrimental to the Country." Hobey argued the affirmative for Cadmean. In 1905-06, St. Paul's organized its first camera club; third-year (Form III) student Hobey Baker was one of its founding members. [15] Shortly after stepping onto campus as a shy 11-year-old boy, Hobey was active and engaged in nearly every facet of school life up in Concord.

What about Hobey's psycho-sexual development? He endured his passage through puberty after losing contact with his mother, surrounded by 320 towel-snapping peers with whom he roomed and showered. By the time he was an upper-class-man, Hobey was a living Adonis who was openly admired for his physical attributes.

"He was very beautifully built for an athlete," said his nephew Hobey II, recalling his father Thornton's description. "Smallish frame, broad shoulders, they looked to him as a promising athlete." [16]

Donald Herring, Hobey's coach and academic advisor at Princeton, was not shy when describing Hobey's appeal to both sexes. "He carried himself with the nonchalant ease of a natural athlete. It was a fact that men liked Hobey as instinctively as did women." [17]

From a Freudian perspective, there was a stabilizing element to Hobey's journey through puberty. Bobby Baker's decision to send his sons to St. Paul's turned out to be a blessing in this case. Master James Conover's wife, known to Hobey as "Aunt Mary," showered him with a mother's love. Mary's son J.P. watched first-hand as the two boys from Philadelphia became his surrogate brothers. "They were treated exactly as members of the family," said J.P. "Mother had to look after them as such, their clothes, their manners, etc. She became fond of them both, especially Hobart, who was more attractive than Thornton, quieter with better manners, and more understanding and considerate of other people." [18]

Mary Conover's bottomless well of maternal love for Hobey was a salve to his emotional wounds emanating from Philadelphia. The first decade of 1900 was one of animus and discord in the Baker family: the parents' separation in 1903, prompting the boys' departure; the scandalous Baker divorce, finalized in 1905; and the boys' father remarrying in 1907, vacating the family home. There can be no doubt that Hobey felt safer in Concord than he did in Philadelphia.

Christmas of 1905, which the Baker brothers shared with the Conovers, generated a pivotal moment in Hobey's life, both athletically and emotionally. In the first month of the 1905-06 hockey season, Hobey's skates were in ruins. He was actually playing on a mixed pair towards the end of December, his family back home unable to afford replacements. One can only imagine Hobey's response when he unwrapped his special present that Christmas morning. Aunt Mary Conover had bequeathed hockey's future king with a new pair of high-end hockey skates! [19] He was out on the ponds before the holiday dinner, heart racing on the black ice. For a boy searching for love, he had found more than a semblance. Oh for the wings of a dove, indeed.

The Conovers were now the boys' full-time family, not only when school was in session, but during Easter break and summer vacations as well. Rather than head home each summer to their crumbling family life in Philadelphia, Hobey and Thornton would join the Conovers in Newport, Rhode Island, half a mile from the beach. "He (Hobey) would spend every day in his bathing suit, no shoes except Sunday." said the younger Conover, "Swam before every meal in the nude, unless there were women around." [20]

Hobey and Thornton visited other relatives during those summers, often in Yorkville, Maine. It was there that Hobey met up with the Roberts twins, proper bachelorettes from Philadelphia. "Thornton was more of a ladies' man than Hobey," said Conover. From all appearances, Hobey enjoyed a healthy relationship with Elizabeth Roberts from age 16 until he graduated from St. Paul's two years later. There are photos of Hobey with the twins, acting as a perfect gentleman and the primary escort for Elizabeth. She actually came to visit Hobey up at St. Paul's over semester break in February of Hobey's upper reserve year, enjoying sleigh rides and cocoa at Hobey's winter cabin getaway, a privileged asset for Hobey's secret society. Roberts, like so many of both sexes, was smitten by Hobey. Despite challenging circumstances, Hobey transitioned through puberty at St. Paul's without crisis, buttressed by Aunt Mary's maternal love. His confidence in affairs of the heart manifested itself in his relationship with Roberts, a friendship colored by mutual respect.

Hobey's devotion to athletics, hockey in particular, became his formula to garner much of the attention he longed for. With only a modicum of training, Hobey could achieve near mastery in any physical endeavor. A star gymnast, he loved impressing others by walking up a flight of stairs while standing on his hands. He was introduced to a pair of roller skates while at St. Paul's, and within minutes was doing tricks and spins on one skate. There was a quarry a short jog from the SPS campus, from which brave students took plunges deep into the chilly swimming hole below. Hobey would climb to the highest rock wall and take majestic 30' swan dives, as well as front and back flips into the depths. According to one Saint Paul's master, "Hobey had perfect control of himself, and could bring every muscle of his body to bear at one time." [21]

Sports historian Stephen Hardy takes issue with those who dismiss Hobey's excellence by implying that his gifts were a product of nature, not nurture, as if his athletic superiority were merely God-given. "To say he was a "natural athlete" is a ruse that entirely misses the point about his greatness," said Hardy. "Hobey had natural ability, but he also had intense dedication that separated him from many of the amateur athletes of his day. Hobey Baker spent endless hours practicing, often by himself. In those formative years at St. Paul's he was by himself, stickhandling in the dark. What better way to learn? He put the time in that a professional athlete would have put in. That's what made him different." [22]

Hobey's athletic brilliance, and his commitment to all the other aspects of the prep school life, made him intensely popular despite his shy nature. His seven years at Saint Paul's had seen him scale the heights of prep culture, and give back as well. During his upper reserve year he not only dominated the sports he competed in, but found time to coach the underclassmen as well. One anecdote by biographer Davies captures the essence of Hobey's sainted life in prep school. His secret club, the Bogue, was hosting a mid-winter dance at which he entertained the two Roberts sisters. After a rousing co-ed pillow fight in the dorms, Hobey exited with his hockey mates and defeated the Boston Crescents club 9-0. Afterward he quickly changed into tux and tails and headed off to the dance, but then he impulsively detoured to the gym. He quickly performed three impeccable giant swings on the high bar. Then he proceeded to the dance, giving his dates from Philadelphia society the time of their lives.[23] This is the stuff of legend—something that might make Jay Gatsby blush.

Not everyone believed that the gilded prep life was ideal, however. Davies points out that 20th Century literary giant Cyrl Connolly, a product of Eton—the British prep school that is the prototype for American church schools like St. Paul's and its peers—cast aspersions on the end product turned out by these all-consuming institutions. He called it the theory of "permanent adolescence."

"It is the theory that the experiences undergone by boys at the great [prep] schools are so intense as to dominate their lives and arrest their development," wrote Connolly. [24] A strong case can be made that Hobey never evolved intellectually or emotionally after St. Paul's. He never acquired the curiosity to grow into anything other than the prep ideal: an educated, well-dressed sportsman who longed for the action of the game. Conforming to the St. Paul's academic tradition of that time, Hobey ignored critical thinking and became a solid, yet uninspired student— he learned how to go along to get along. Hobey's friends from Saint Paul's always held the highest status in Hobey's personal life, more so than any future acquaintances.

Immersed in activities with his new St. Paul's family, interaction with his biological brood down in Philadelphia was limited to occasional letter writing; personal visits were a rarity. Then midway through the 1908-09 school year, in what the two brothers thought was their Form VI send-off to college, Hobey and Thornton received another bombshell from Philadelphia.

Their father, now living in the family home of his new wife Laura Butcher Baker, had become strapped financially due to the Wall Street crash known as the "Bankers' Panic of 1907." With his upholstery business hanging by a thread, Alfred Baker's dwindling funds could only support one of his sons' college aspirations. And whoever the boy was, he would be forced to wait an additional year for father to get his finances in order. It was here that the gallant Thornton set aside his own dreams in order to allow Hobey's star to continue its ascent over Princeton. Thornton was a good enough athlete to make varsity hockey his senior year as a reserve; Hobey was captain for three seasons and superstar for four. Older brother deferred to the younger prodigy.

"My dad's reasoning was Hobey will be the one who will star," said Thornton's son Hobey II, who then quoted his father. "He'll be the famed one at Princeton, I'd rather give him the opportunity to do that. I'm not nearly the athlete my brother is. Let Hobey have the opportunity at Princeton, and be the athlete we know he can be." [25]

It was an immensely powerful gesture by Thornton, one that Hobey never fully reconciled, a debt of gratitude that would trail younger brother for the rest of his life. In addition to Thornton's beau geste, Hobey's self-esteem was wounded by an assortment of unsettling developments. He may have been voted the best athlete his last three years at St. Paul's, but internally he was haunted by a troubling sequence of events: his parents' divorce, his mother being institutionalized, the loss of the family fortune, and now his brother forfeiting his college dreams on account of him. During his Form VI and post-graduate year at St. Paul's, Hobey felt like a paper tiger, surrounded by America's wealthiest heirs at the most prestigious prep school in the country. Older brother Thornton, whom he idolized, set about to rebuild the family's failing business, all so his younger sibling could continue on his path to glory on the playing fields of Princeton. Hobey graduated from St. Paul's in June of 1910 as the most polished sportsman ever to matriculate to Princeton, yet he harbored unspeakable secrets and an ever-widening hole in his fragile psyche.

A modern look across Lower School Pond at St. Paul's School in Concord, N.H., virtually identical to what Hobey witnessed from 1903–1910. (Tim Rappleye)

HOBEYQUEST:
THE SCHLEY BROTHERS

It was my good fortune to have met the hockey-playing Schley brothers, Reeve and John, as fellow Winter Club members in the 1980's. They are two of nine Schley relatives who all attended St. Paul's, spanning the years from 1937 to 1999. Reeve graduated from St. Paul's in 1954, the last class to have used the Lower School Pond as its exclusive hockey venue. Due to warming winters and the introduction of milfoil algae into the ponds, maintaining outdoor ice became a losing battle at St. Paul's. Magazines and pamphlets show the lengths the SPS maintenance chiefs would go to preserve their precious ice, hoisting 40' high canvas sheets to prevent the sun from wreaking its late-winter havoc. The SPS hockey dynasty began its decline when it systematically transitioned to artificial ice with the 1954 building of Gordon Rink, constructed on solid ground.

The Schley brothers, still active as 80-year-olds, served as oral historians for their school's famous hockey program. It was St. Paul's that scratched out America's first rules of hockey in December of 1884, and hosted the country's first formal game 12 years later. Because of St. Paul's consistent production of elite college players in the early 20th century, it became rightly known as "The Cradle of American Hockey." Reeve Schley III recalled spending many afternoons on the second floor of the SPS library, looking down the length of Lower School Pond and seeing most of the school on blades. "I'd be in study hall and look out, and see 500 kids skating. Once lunch was over, you could play all afternoon long." In the Saint Paul's glory days, as many as 33 intramural teams could practice or play games each afternoon.

While speaking on the phone, Reeve mentioned that he was looking at a photo of the 1900-01 St. Paul's varsity, and he began reciting its remarkable won-loss record. "They beat Harvard and Yale varsities that year," said Schley proudly. He mentioned that the SPS captain, future Harvard football stalwart Philip Overton Mills, had been one of the many St. Paul's men to die in World War I. A visit to the comprehensive SPS on-line archives quickly confirmed Schley's precise recollection.

Reeve patiently explained to me how St. Paul's Turkey Pond and Lower School Pond were two different bodies, and how SPS hockey players preferred getting a ride to Turkey Pond, a half mile off the main campus past an old farm. He explained its hockey significance: how the shallowness of Turkey Pond made it the earliest venue suitable for skating each year, usually in November. Elite players and young prodigies often accompanied their masters for those early-season skates.

The SPS hockey "factory" was no secret; it was featured in a three-page magazine spread in the December 1916 issue of Country Life in America, complemented by several photos including a shot of Hobey Baker posing in full gear, with the caption "America's Greatest Hockey Player." Forty years later, Sports Illustrated published a lengthy spread devoted to SPS Hockey titled "Schoolboy Hockey Boom." This story contains large color photos of cheering crowds surrounding one of the seven rinks on the Lower School Pond. This was toward the end of the SPS hockey glory days, a dynasty that ended in 1966 with the covering of Gordon Rink, when their hockey operation moved inside full time. Scheduling all its teams onto one formal ice surface upended St. Paul's winning formula of nearly limitless ice time, and their varsity hockey team soon slid back into the pack with its prep school siblings.

Tracing the origins of a century-old hockey icon can be challenging, and I was quite fortunate to have John Schley share with me his "Homeric" history of Hobey Baker. Baker's former SPS captain, Howell "Patsy" Campbell, never left Saint Paul's, returning as a teacher, coach and administrator in his later years. He oversaw the SPS lunch room in John Schley's Form II year (8th grade) in 1952, and Schley remembers Campbell scolding him for not washing behind his ears. Campbell then brought up the topic of Hobey Baker to the hockey-loving prep. The younger Schley brother, who went on to star for Yale, was eager to learn all he could about the legendary Baker. Campbell added a walking tour to his lecture, and escorted the 13-year-old Schley out along the wooded paths near the shore of Lower School Pond, where he eventually revealed Hobey's secret hiding spot for his skates. Campbell died a year later, but not before passing on the tasty nugget from Baker's life in hockey's cradle to Schley, who fed me, and it is now in print; two fabulous assists on the score.

The trails along St. Paul's Lower School Pond are part of the lore of Hobey Baker. The late hockey author Jack Falla hiked that trail, as did sports historian Stephen Hardy from the University of New Hampshire. Hardy considers his trip around the pond a "sacred walk." On a research mission to Concord in 2017, I wandered the SPS campus and found myself drawn to the pond, and then to its trail. The only signs of human life were the blazes on the birch and pine trees framing the path. It didn't take me long to realize that I was on Hobey's turf, and I stopped to shoot a photo across the pond. I focused on the tall spires of the Chapel of Peter and St. Paul's. This was the identical vista that Hobey had taken in when he stashed his skates over a century ago.

I returned to the trail, examining the trees and their roots, scoping their proximity to the shore. A hundred yards later

I halted in my tracks. There was a giant white sycamore, with large exposed roots just a few paces from the water. In my mind I had found it, the ideal tree for Hobey to have hidden his skates. I stared out at the pond, and tried to imagine what it was like at night, in pitch dark. This is where Hobey had perfected his Hall of Fame skill—stick-handling a puck blinded by the night. Hardy's assertion was spot-on: this was indeed a sacred walk.

CHAPTER THREE

Hockey Purgatory

Hobey Baker arrived at Princeton in the fall of 1910, tan, fit, and surrounded by his best friends. He proceeded directly to Nassau Street, where he reconvened with Wendel Kuhn, Thornton Emmons, Ehrich Kilmer, and two other Saint Paul's chums at a large apartment, one floor above Renwick's restaurant. This would be Baker's home for much of his college career. It was known to this preppy sextet as the "Sweat Pea," in honor of their much-loved boarding school. Despite being a raw college freshman, Hobey was in his comfort zone at Princeton: his great uncle Alfred was the esteemed rector of Princeton's Trinity Church, and 244 of his incoming class of 325 came from prep schools. Classmates who were familiar with the prep sports scene were certainly aware of Hobey Baker.

His hockey reputation clearly preceded him; after all, his St. Paul's hockey club had defeated Princeton's varsity, the intercollegiate champs, earlier that year. He had practiced informally with, and scrimmaged against, the Tigers on Lake Carnegie several times in recent years. There was no doubt that he would fit right into their lineup when the time came. But that time was well over a year away; unlike Harvard or Yale, Princeton had no freshman team. Hobey would have to "go it alone," for an additional 15 months, enduring his entire freshman year and part of the next without the security of "hockey player" as his primary identity.

To most students at Ol' Nassau, *football* was the sport. Compared to Ivy League football spectacles at University Field, Princeton varsity hockey games were but an afterthought, played 50 miles north in Manhattan. If Hobey wanted to establish a name for himself on this campus, he would have to do it on Princeton's local gridiron.

Football fields were no place for boys in the early 20th century. According to the *Washington Post,* 45 players died playing football between 1900 and 1905, twenty in 1905 alone. [1] Two-hundred pound linemen stacked the line of scrimmage and mauled helpless running backs in their attempts to break through for positive yardage. Prior to 1906 there were no rules against punching, kicking or head-breaking in those lethal scrums. Had the 160-pound Hobey tried to play college football five years earlier, he would have been broken like dry kindling.

Finally, President Teddy Roosevelt stepped in. During the 1905 season, his son Teddy, Jr. had been bullied and bloodied in a Harvard freshman game, and Teddy, Sr. had seen enough. He rounded up college football's ruling powers and put them together in one room, demanding that rules be changed to save the sport that was so important to him and the rest of the country. [2] By the time Hobey tried out for freshman football in the autumn of 1910, the deadly "Flying V" formation had been outlawed, limits had been placed on the number of men on the line, and the forward pass legalized. This modified version of the game was now suitable for a smaller man like Baker. Consistently throwing the ball, however, was still over a decade away, repudiated by football's stodgy eastern faction.

If you look at photos from Hobey's era, the football looks more like a pumpkin than the oblong sphere it is today. Due to the ball's shape and stubborn tradition, football in 1910 was a kickers' game—punting and drop-kick field goals prevailed. Eastern schools were the most conservative and unimaginative teams in the nation. Harvard versus Yale, known as "The Game" then and now, finished as scoreless ties in both 1910 and 1911. Wary of turnovers, Ivy league teams often chose to punt on first down, turning football into a game of cautious field position. This version of football, with so much emphasis on kicking and returning punts, now had room for a quick cat like Hobey.

Despite college football's lack of scoring, it remained insanely popular in America, hyped relentlessly by the plethora of big city newspapers. Ivy League football became a see-and-be-seen spectacle, prompting thousands of spectators to jam into trains headed to New York, Boston, New Haven, and Princeton on Saturdays, all desperate to see America's toughest young gentlemen slug it out on the gridiron.

Princeton's football practices were run by the "committee system," in which a recently graduated star player would assume the head coaching duties, and a cadre of good ol' boys would be the assistants. Hobey never had the same head football coach twice while playing at Princeton. Eastern schools dismissed the forward pass as a gimmick, nearly ignoring offense altogether. The Princeton game plans consisted of three running plays—left, right and center. The coaches had never seen the likes of Hobey, not only his speed, coordination and creativity, but also his work ethic. After each practice, Hobey would "take footballs up and down the sidelines, kicking field goals from every five-yard stripe." [3] Baker soon secured a spot as both the place kicker and the sure-handed punt returner for the freshmen, the most important positions on the field back in the day.

Although the freshman team garnered little attention compared to the varsity, everyone on campus knew the importance of the Yale game, a team the Princeton frosh had not beaten in recent memory. Hobey recorded the first entry into his legendary Princeton sports "scrapbook" in the Tigers' 6-0 victory over the rival Elis. Toward the end of a scoreless game, he unilaterally chose to fake a field goal, and then charted a course downfield. The goal line was 20 yards away, but Hobey must have run at least twice that distance, tacking and jibing, zigging and zagging, repeatedly dodging would-be tacklers. Eyewitnesses recalled Hobey pausing for his blockers, and then revving up his motor again to elude his blue-clad pursuers en route to the end zone. Hobey's jolt of unshackled athleticism resulted in the game's only score, and it left the Princeton contingent giddy, if not confused, in the joyous aftermath. No one had ever seen such combined speed and elusive guile on the gridiron. It transformed another boring scoreless tie into an electrifying win over Yale, something no Tiger on campus had experienced. It was the inauguration of the Hobey Baker Era of Princeton athletics.

This previously Neanderthal sport had just been injected with a heaping dose of Hobey's feline agility, a veritable Princeton Tiger. "When football first evolved, it was a plodding game," said Jerry Price, Princeton's long-time sports communications director. "Someone like Hobey Baker, an athlete of great grace and great speed—but not size—stood out from that mold. He was able to bring a degree of artistry that other people couldn't bring." [4]

The artist as a young man may have been a lightweight, but Hobey used football to harden his amazing physique. Old-school coaches have always sought players brave enough to run through brick walls, or in early 20th century football, run into the mass of humanity that was the front line, and accept the subsequent kicks and punches. Hobey was both willing and able. For all his publicity gained as a brilliant open-field runner and kicker, he was also the primary running back on those Princeton squads. He was frequently called upon to sprint into the immovable wall of linemen, more than any other player, only to be body-slammed down with cartoon violence. Newspaper accounts and dozens of anecdotes are unanimous in their descriptions of

Hobey, how he would bounce up from those jarring hits, often with a smile on his face, seemingly eager to return for more. Baker prepared his body for those weekly assaults with ritual exercise, adhering to a strict routine he developed at St. Paul's. Aware that his neck was narrower than his teammates, Hobey devoted long hours of work in the dorm to compensate, performing innovative exercises specifically designed to broaden his neck. As screenwriter Bruce Smith pointed out, Baker was a driven man.

Without hockey to play his freshman year, Hobey sampled numerous other sports after football season: gymnastics, swimming, riflery, golf, and tennis. He opted for baseball in the spring and was the best ball-hawk in Princeton's freshman outfield. With just minimal instruction, Baker excelled at them all. "Had he had the time," said football assistant Donald Herring, "he might have played on five varsity teams in any one year." [5]

One hundred fifty miles east, a Native American was wowing the Carlisle Indian Industrial School in rural Pennsylvania. Like Baker, Jim Thorpe was a master of every sport his college offered: track, baseball, basketball, boxing and tennis, not to mention football. The biggest contrast between the two men was in their dress: Baker was never without his Norfolk jacket and linen pants; Thorpe's wardrobe was strictly blue collar. Without clothes, however, their differences melted away. The best description Hobey's coach Herring could come up with for Baker's magnificent physique was that of a Blackfoot Indian on display at Chicago's Field Museum. [6]

As all-around athletes, the two men both had gilded sports resumes: Hobey gained membership into both the Hockey and College Football Halls of Fame; Thorpe was a star football and baseball player, and a gold medal Olympic decathlete. They were by far America's most gifted athletes of their era, the equivalent of two Bo Jacksons playing at the same time. In the 1911-12 school year, Baker won national championships in two different sports at Princeton. Thorpe, on the other hand, was anointed "the greatest athlete in the world" at the 1912 Olympic Games in Stockholm. Then he headed back to Carlisle that fall where he joined Baker on the All-American team as a halfback. Ultimately, the issue that separated these two superstars was their philosophy towards professionalism—Thorpe needed money during his college years, receiving cash to play semi-pro baseball; the aristocratic Baker thought professionalism abhorrent.

When Baker returned to Princeton for his sophomore year in the fall of 1911, his sports smorgasbord came to an end. Princeton allowed its varsity athletes to play only *two* sports, so Hobey was forced to whittle his choices down to hockey and one other. Many of his peers believed Baker would have made a top-flight baseball outfielder, and he swam like "a machine," but Hobey chose football.

In hindsight, it was an obvious choice. Both hockey and football have the element of high-stakes keep-away; whether it be ball or puck, fans can't take their eyes off the performer in possession. Baker, like so many sons deprived of a mother's love, thrived on attention to fill that void. But his individual forays with puck and pigskin came at a steep price. Players that possess the objects of desire in big-time contact sports become human targets, especially hockey and football where intimidation is a common tactic. Baker's devotion to hardening his body for frequent attacks, along with his incredible reflexes, may explain why he was never seriously injured over his career. The man, however, was punished mercilessly when opponents finally tracked him down. Hobey never filled his emotional void, and never ceased seeking out the ball or the puck, despite the repeated pounding.

In the fall of 1911, the Baker sports legend had still not been cemented at Princeton. There were loud whispers from St. Paul's grads, and from those who had seen him skate in New York, about the hockey phenom in waiting, but Hobey was hardly the big man on campus. It was not a given that he would even make the varsity football team. He was, after all, the lightest man going out for the squad—this in a sport that valued manly bulk and aggression above all else. "A light guy like me is almost certain to get hurt and not last very long," said Baker, in his typically modest style. [7]

But Hobey possessed far too much talent to be ignored, even by the unscientific Princeton football staff. They had seen Baker handle punts flawlessly for the freshman squad in 1910, so they gave him a shot at the varsity as a sophomore. When Hobey wove his way through heavy traffic for a lengthy punt-return touchdown on opening day, no one would ever again question Hobey's football status; he was a fixture from that point forward.

The 1911 season was a curious one for Princeton: despite record books declaring them consensus national champions, they were hardly a dominant force. Hosting Harvard, they managed but a single first down offensively. With teenager F. Scott Fitzgerald in the house, it was Princeton's star *defensive* end Sanford White who provided the offensive fireworks, scooping up a blocked field goal and rumbling 95 yards for the score. Fitzgerald was one of the 22,000 delirious fans at Princeton's University Field that Saturday. "Sam White decides me for Princeton!" wrote Fitzgerald, who was contemplating colleges at the time. [8]

The remainder of that afternoon was a punt-fest, and Hobey fielded his numerous chances flawlessly. Harvard's returner, on the other hand, misjudged a crucial punt due to the gusting winds, resulting in a two-point safety for the Tigers. Those points became critical, especially when Harvard positioned itself for a rare touchdown with an even rarer long pass. Going into the game, Harvard was the consensus top team in the country, but White's heroics and Hobey's impeccable handling of wind-driven punts helped seal the upset for Princeton at Ol' Nassau.

Knocked from their perch atop the college football world, Harvard next played a school not easily recognized by the Hearst (*New York Journal*) and Pulitzer (*New York World*) broad sheets—Carlisle Indian Industrial School. A group of Native Americans shocked the snooty Crimson 18-15. One man scored every point for the Indians via a touchdown and four field goals—a flat-nosed 200-pound brute of a man named Jim Thorpe. Hearst and Pulitzer had found themselves a compelling new character to help sell their papers. A single loss kept the Carlisle Indians out of the national championship picture, but Thorpe's dominance was impossible to ignore, and he gained a headline spot on Walter Camp's 1911 All-American team.

The Tigers escaped their own upset that week with a tight 3-0 victory over Dartmouth, setting the stage for a crucial show-down with Yale to cap the season. If they could manage to beat the 7-1 Elis, Princeton would stay undefeated on the year and claim the intercollegiate championship. But this was no fait accompli; the Bulldogs practically owned the Tigers, having not lost to Princeton in eight years.

Instead of the high winds from the Harvard game, the national championship showdown in New Haven was subject to a more menacing version of mother nature—torrential downpours. The game ball, a swollen pigskin, was now of the greased variety. Yale's normally sure-handed safety, all-American captain Art Howe, fumbled away that slick pig four times. Hobey, however, secured every tricky punt and helped improve the Tigers field position with returns averaging nearly 15 yards, somehow maintaining possession each time. As a halfback, he had his number called repeatedly, getting walloped time and again by Yale's All-American end Doug Bomeisler. One eyewitness exclaimed, "Why he (Hobey) wasn't killed, I don't know." [9]

Once again, Princeton generated offense from their defense, as the heroic Sanford White scored on yet another long fumble return, sloshing 68 yards through the New Haven muck for Princeton's only points. Yale converted only one of eight field goal attempts, and Princeton won the muddy war. As champions of the Big Three—Harvard-Yale-Princeton—the Tigers were anointed national champions by the opinion shapers of the day, the inky press. Hobey was once again flawless, if not spectacular, in his role as punt returner. Safely fielding every punt was a singular feat in those horrendous conditions. He caught the eye of several newspapermen who had weathered the storm in New Haven. "A man who could not have been spared," was the description of Hobey in one game story, which also declared that Hobey held "...a very high place in the admiration of the spectators." [10]

There is no doubt that this sophomore, the lightest man on the field, was an undeniable factor in college football's nascent national championship game. Hobey had become a major force in America's most popular sport.

Princeton's post game celebration was a muddy maelstrom, players unrecognizable from the black sludge obscuring their faces, hugging each other in teary reverie. Champagne flowed, men burst out in song, delirium reigned. Generations of Princeton men had long awaited this moment: a national championship, and just as importantly, a victory over blood-rival Yale. There in the midst of the muck and the mire, stood Hobey— showered and dressed, a pair of skates hanging around his neck. He was soberly seeking a ride to the New Haven train station. What in God's name was he doing? "Saint Nick's is opening tonight," said Baker, "and I'd like to get in some skating." [11]

Teammates stared in disbelief. To many of the drained players, this was the pinnacle of their lives, certainly their zenith as college athletes. Hobey, however, had a different paradigm. Despite appearances, Hobey's dash out of the national championship locker room wasn't illogical. To Baker, football was merely a fill, in this case a damn long one, until hockey season. It had been nearly two years since the "king of hockey" had played a formal game on ice. His request to play for the St. Nick's club his freshman year had been denied by the Princeton administrators. To Hobey, the business of football was just that: carefully fielding punts and applying his drop-kicking craft with an educated toe, all to keep the low-scoring Tigers on pace with their opponents. The sport had no creativity on offense, and little outlet for Hobey's abundant athletic genius.

His two years of hockey purgatory were now over, and Hobey was determined to catch that train to Grand Central Station. From there it was a quick shot over to Saint Nicholas Arena on 66th and Columbus. He could finally leave the blubbering brutes, the muddy quagmire, and the archaic rules of football behind. Hobey dashed from the din without looking back. He had scored a ride and was off to his frozen mecca, and a clean sheet of ice.

There is a bittersweet footnote to that undefeated football season. The 1911 Princeton Tigers were honored as "National Champions," having earned that title courtesy of Messrs. Pulitzer, Hearst, and the rest of the eastern press. The team celebrated in fine style at the Princeton Club in Philadelphia, an easy commute for former Tigers running back Bobby Baker. Proud Papa beamed when the team was presented with shiny gifts to commemorate their championship season. Dad limped up to join his son at the podium, as toastmaster Lou Reichner teased father and son. "I have nothing for Papa Baker," said Lou to the well-lubricated crowd, who all knew of the old man's reputation as a star halfback in the 1880's. Reichner then presented Hobey with his gold cufflinks. "If father is man enough to take them from his son, he can have them!" and the room roared with a triple cheer. [12]

Hobey couldn't help noticing the senior Baker wince in pain when they returned to their table, and how frustrated his father became trying to manage his cutlery all night. At the end of the evening Hobey had to help the 48-year-old man into the waiting car. The senior Baker's motor skills never stopped deteriorating over the remainder of his shortened life.

CHAPTER FOUR

Here He Comes!

For Hobey Baker, New York City was an integral part of his hockey experience. He was a performer who fed off the roaring crowds that filled Princeton's home rink—Saint Nicholas Arena in the heart of Manhattan. Situated a block from Broadway on West 66th Street and Columbus Avenue, the arena known as Saint Nick's was the predecessor of today's Madison Square Garden. Hobey knew the venue well, having played Christmas holiday events there for four years while at St. Paul's, and occasionally practicing with New York's best amateur team—St. Nick's—during his "hockey purgatory" freshman year at Princeton. During his three seasons of college hockey and two for St. Nick's following graduation, Hobey amassed a five-year string of individual athletic dominance that was comparable to Dodgers pitching legend Sandy Koufax during his abbreviated Major League prime. Hockey superstar Bobby Orr played a shade under ten professional seasons, but he too was a sporting comet: brilliant, impossible to ignore, and short lived.

"Hobey Baker by far was the first American superstar in the New York area," said Stan Fischler, the man known as the "Hockey Maven," who has been covering the sport intensely since the 1940's. "The hockey hotbed, Saint Nicholas Arena, was located right across from where Lincoln Center is today, Broadway and Columbus. There was no arena that was bigger." [1]

Because Princeton played all its home games 50 miles north of campus at Saint Nicholas Arena, the reality was that Hobey the hockey player was a New York sports treasure—he just happened to wear the Princeton sweater for three of his glory years. He developed a legion of New York fans, and the managers of the arena, operating a mere block from Broadway, discovered that Hobey's name on the marquee translated to ticket sales. In the early 20th century, Saint Nicholas Arena was known for staging fights as well as hockey games. The boxing business was handled by the McMahon brothers, Eddie and Jess. Hockey was managed primarily by Cornelius Fellowes, a New Yorker whose passion for pucks was surpassed only by his appreciation for swift thoroughbreds. Jess McMahon's son would later surpass them all as sports promoters—the infamous Vince McMahon of professional wrestling. Back in December of 1911, it did not take these three well-heeled "sportsmen" long to realize that Baker's box office appeal would significantly fatten their wallets.

As America made the turn into the 20th century, its sports fans needed something to fill the void in the cold months after baseball season. The occasional horse race or prize fight wasn't enough to satisfy the sports hunger of America's growing population centers, particularly on the east coast. First came college football, with its four-year cycles of unpaid amateur athletes competing every autumn Saturday; it soon sprinted to the top of the spectator pyramid. And thanks to Saint Nicholas Arena, it was hockey that bridged New York's live sports void from Thanksgiving until pitchers and catchers reported to Major League spring training camps each March. "Since there was no National Hockey League even born until the next to last year of Hobey's life, college hockey was the thing," said Fischler. "It was big stuff."

Like football, the sport of hockey at the beginning of the 20th century would be hard to recognize today. The two biggest differences were 1) in addition to the goalies, there were six skaters per side, not five; and 2) forward passes were illegal. Goalies wore less padding than 21st century forwards do today, and no one wore helmets. The game was ripe for a player who could outskate the pack while handling the puck; Hobey was a master at both.

In the early 1900's, players' skates were like short skis, difficult to maneuver, and each change of direction required two-skate perpendicular braking. Not for Hobey. His custom rockered skates and lightning reflexes allowed him to change directions instantaneously, spinning on his toes to jet away from would-be defenders. Teammates could not keep up with him, so there was little use in Hobey passing the puck until he ventured deep into the attacking zone.

Hobey's teams had three forwards and two defensemen like they do today, but with one additional position, which no longer exists. It is called the "Rover," a position that appeared to have been designed explicitly for Baker. It allowed and encouraged him to do exactly that, *rove* around the ice, something he did non-stop, usually in possession of the puck. To get a sense of Hobey's dominance on ice, one can search YouTube for video clips of Bobby Orr playing for the NHL Bruins in the early 1970's. Orr's rink-length rushes were Hobey's signature, along with the accompanying cry of "Here he comes!" This was shouted by delirious crowds, home and away, on both sides of the Canadian border. Some of Bobby Orr's most amazing highlights—collecting a stick from the bench in mid-rush, creating outrageous scoring plays while flat on his back—were being performed by Hobey 60 years prior. Sellout crowds, and the profit-hungry promoters, became ecstatic.

Hobey's explosive arrival on the Manhattan scene created

a new generation of sporting fans from society's upper crust. Lawrence Perry of the *New York Evening Post* set the stage for a typical Hobey game-night:

> *Long lines of limousines and carriages backed up all the way to Central Park, a fashionable audience in evening dress, all to see Baker play. When he got the puck for a long dash the cheering grew hysterical, and there were bursts of applause a hundred times a night—of a sort the reporter had never heard before.* [2]

It is impossible to know what was going through Hobey's mind prior to his long-anticipated first game for the Princeton Tigers in the final days of December, 1911. A month prior to his 20th birthday, Hobey had taken the train up to Manhattan, and was likely tinkering with his skates in the home locker room, quiet in the final moments prior to puck drop. Hobey was now a man, body hardened from two bruising seasons of college football. He had not played a formal game of hockey since his final year at St. Paul's, 21 months prior.

It was a full house that night at Saint Nicholas Arena, 4,000 fans eager to see the much-heralded star and his Princeton mates take on Williams College, the season-opener for both clubs. Prior to the game, the team from the small school in western Massachusetts was described as "formidable." [3] Based on Hobey's hockey wizardry, it is doubtful that he was nervous, more likely a man immersed in eager anticipation, a young colt bucking to get out of the barn and run.

That is exactly what he became, a whirling dervish against the outclassed Williams skaters. Hobey riddled the Ephs with half a dozen goals, and piled on three more assists in a 14-0 rout. Baker thrived on clean sheets of ice: it allowed him to skate full tilt with the puck on his stick, with no accumulated snow to infringe on his precise control. He was a force this night, literally skating rings around the opposition.

Much like NBA superstar Michael Jordan, who had Scottie Pippen to run with him and share the offensive load, Hobey had classmate Wendel Kuhn at his side on every wrung of his hockey ladder—St. Paul's, Princeton, and St. Nick's. The lanky Kuhn had great reach, skated his lane reliably, and was a deadly shooter. The two men's signature scoring play was for Hobey to dash deep into the offensive zone, past the enemy goal line. Just as he was about to crash into the far end boards, Hobey would fire a pass to his pal Kuhn, having just arrived at the goalmouth. Kuhn would blast the puck past the overwhelmed goalie, and the rout would be on.

Princeton had tied for last place in the 1910–11 season, but all that changed with the arrival of gold-dust twins Baker and Kuhn. There is no doubt that Hobey was the center of attention because he spent so much time possessing the puck. Their trips to Boston became a spectacle, thanks to the new Boston Arena, a 6,000-seat state of the art venue that opened in 1910, one year before Hobey's first game for Princeton. Unlike the crowd of excited gentiles in New York, Boston Arena contained the bawdiest and most knowledgeable hockey crowds in America. Jammed into the Arena's prominent balconies, Boston hockey fans filled their shiny new arena to the rafters to see Hobey play, whether it be against Harvard, the Boston Crescents, or the Boston Athletic Association.

It mattered not that he was on the opposing team, fans in the Hub of Hockey were mad for Hobey the way one might appreciate a concert pianist or the dancing of Baryshnikov. Harvard star Stuart Kaiser spoke for all of Baker's opponents. "This was no enemy we were watching, we were looking at an unparalleled feat of magic artistry." [4] But unlike a formal night at the opera, rabid Boston hockey fans lost their minds and their collective voices when Hobey would round the net for his signature forays down the ice. Such roaring adulation, both in Boston and New York, clearly had an effect on Hobey's internal chemistry.

The only amateur American player who can be legitimately compared to Hobey is Harvard legend Bill Cleary, another man who knows what it's like to bring fans out of their seats while carrying the puck. Like Baker, Cleary played dozens of his college games at Boston Arena under its steep balconies. New England-based hockey aficionado Stephen Hardy knows and loves Cleary, and chuckles at the recollection of his signature battle cry, "Give me the Goddam puck!"

"You could see a crescendo in the crowd," said Cleary, reminiscing about his heroics from both college and two sets of Olympic Winter Games. "The roar would start, and you're subconsciously aware of that. And you know you have that ability to *do it*, to split the defense and score." [5] Cleary gets red in the face, balling his 80-year old hands into fists during his flashback to the glory days.

Cleary provides the best guess as to what Hobey felt when he was winding up for one of his patented rushes in America's two biggest hockey venues. One of those, Boston Arena, is still around today, now known as Matthews Arena, the home of the NCAA Northeastern Huskies. The century-old hockey barn still has its iconic balconies, virtually hanging over the playing surface. Photographs of Saint Nicholas Arena reveal its own low-hanging balconies framing the ice. Those special seats allowed the fans to closely track every stride of Hobey's fantastic journeys down the ice, and provide the rolling thunder that gave him jolts of adrenaline.

In Baker's letters home from World War I, he describes the "thrill" he got from aerial dogfights, comparing them to his athletic endeavors. There is no doubt he got an intense rush from the high-speed action of hockey and open-field running in football. His "fight-or-flight" brain chemicals would be secreting in full force during his "sorties," while making instantaneous responses to would-be assailants. Many of those rushes resulted in goals, with the ensuing explosive celebrations. Modern neuroscientists have equated these sports highs with those of recreational drugs. [6] And as Cleary states, they are intensified by the crescendo of roaring fans, especially in those enclosed arenas which became echo chambers. Hysterical crowds provided the sound track for Hobey's game, as fan mania followed him down the ice from directly overhead. The Saint Nicholas and Boston Arenas became neural laboratories of sorts, where Hobey's brain was rewired by the morphine receptors and neuro-transmitters that flooded his system for hours at a time.

There was no formal tracking of athletes' cardiovascular capacity in the early 20th century, but there is ample anecdotal evidence that Hobey's heart and lungs could propel him longer, farther and faster than any of his athletic peers. A football teammate recalled an evening's tactical session in the gym following a grueling workout on the gridiron. "Here we are with our tails dragging from afternoon practice," said the fellow Tiger, "and what is Hobey doing but giant swings on the horizontal bar. Looking at him wears me out." [7]

Hockey games consisted of 40-minutes of regulation play back in Hobey's day; there was no changing on the fly once shifts extended past forty seconds. Substitutions were rare, similar to today's soccer. In all the biographical material on Baker, no one ever recalls him being substituted for, except for the rare injury. He was an iron man who ran at full throttle, all game, every game. Following the 14-0 blowout of Williams that kicked off his college career, the Tigers hung an identical score on Dartmouth. Their 28 goals of offense represented production the Princeton football team could only dream about. Finally able to get on the ice wearing the school's signature orange stripes, this was a Tiger unchained. A season after finishing in last place,

Princeton was propelled to the 1912 intercollegiate championship by Hobey and company.

New York was a newspaper town, expanding fans' appetites, and then feeding its readership the entertainment it now hungered for. As boxing specialists, the McMahon brothers knew that it was the individual athlete, more than teams, that put fannies in the seats. Hobey was the toast of the town in short order, a role in which he was not entirely comfortable. He received an inordinate amount of newsprint, as headlines such as "Plain Case of Too Much Baker," "Baker Does it Again," and "Baker Rescues Tigers from Defeat," had become commonplace. [8]

Our neighbors to the north were the original purveyors of hockey hyperbole. The sport has been Canada's religion ever since it invented hockey in the early 19th century. A player of Hobey's caliber and reputation could never escape the watchful eye of hockey's passionate caretakers, regardless of his nationality. As both Princeton and Hobey's hockey stature exploded during Baker's junior year, the Tigers were invited north to play McGill University in Montreal. The best analogy as to how vital hockey is to the population of Montreal is to imagine São Paulo, Brazil, during the heyday of soccer immortal Pele.

The young fans of Montreal swarmed Princeton's train when it pulled into Montreal. Hobey and his teammates, groggy from the overnight ride, couldn't quite believe the reception, as the chant of "Hobey, Hobey, Hobey!" greeted their arrival. Soon young fans surrounded Baker, begging for an autograph, or better yet, a stick. Baker was reticent, but gracious. [9] His teammates who lived long enough to witness Beatle-mania, already knew what it was like to travel with a sensational rock star.

On the ice, Baker was a relentless perfectionist, driven like no other college hockey player of his day. He was having several pairs of his skates sent back and forth via train to New Hampshire, up to his trusted St. Paul's trainer Johnny Mack, who tuned his blades to perfection and then shipped them back. He had the St. Nicholas maintenance workers kill the lights so he could continue his practice of stick-handling in the dark. The core of Hobey's athletic greatness was as much perspiration as it was inspiration.

"It's hard to be a great athlete," said Princeton sports information director (SID) Jerry Price in his description of Hobey. "You have to have talent, you have to work to develop it, you have to be willing to give up other things that people have. You have to be willing to deal with failure, you have to be willing to deal with pain, you have to be willing to take your shot at being great. That's the lure of athletics." [10]

In the late 1950's, John Davies and Hobey's nephew Henry canvassed all living players from Hobey's era 40 years after his death, amassing anecdotes to help transmit the Baker legend from memory to words on paper. One of the best tales is when Princeton played the truculent Irish American Athletic Association (IAA) club at Saint Nick's Arena. Hobey got checked high into the boards, and actually found his footing atop the dasher. Witnesses swear that he maintained his speed by running along the top of the boards, inches from the astonished fans, and then returning to the ice 20 feet further along, dropping down to reclaim possession of the puck. He continued on to score a miraculous goal that added to his legend. [11]

Players and fans lucky enough to witness Hobey's impossible grace have remembered it their entire lives. Holbrook Cushing was the Princeton Hockey captain three years after Hobey graduated, a man who skated in Hobey's jetstream at St. Paul's and St. Nick's as well. "I had 16 years of hockey, and I never saw anyone who could skate like him," said Cushing, who like so many others, fell in love with Hobey's élan. "More graceful than any dancer, like a bird soaring. His coordination was a gift from heaven, very beautiful." [12]

There were stories of games at Boston Arena that grew so

loud that the referees were forced to use hand signals because their whistles would go unnoticed in the din. Another astonishing highlight came during a game against rival Yale, when Hobey was tripped as he closed in on goal. While sliding on his chest, Hobey managed to fire the puck into the goal. It foreshadowed the NHL's greatest video highlight—a goal scored a century later by Russian-born Alexander Ovechkin while flat on his back. Ovechkin's goal has been viewed tens of thousands of times thanks to modern technology. Hobey's highlight simply requires one's imagination.

But there were just as many anecdotes about Hobey's bighearted sportsmanship as there were about his playing heroics. During an informal scrimmage on Lake Carnegie, the back of Hobey's skate accidentally gashed freshman Jim Deckert's shin. Hobey made a point of visiting Deckert in the infirmary twice-a-day, every day, until he healed. Or the night Yale extended Princeton to overtime, and Eli forward Charles Dickey was whistled off for tripping Hobey. Dickey was an old teammate of Baker's from St. Paul's, and Baker felt terrible for his chum, believing that the infraction was purely accidental. Despite it being overtime, with the game on the line, Hobey made his case to disallow the penalty. "He was playing the puck, not me," said Hobey in his passionate appeal. "That penalty could cost them the game!" Such pleas were a first for the official, who threw up his hands and acquiesced. [13] Hobey himself was whistled off for but a single penalty in his three-year college career, when a Williams skater tripped over his stick.

Due to the proximity of both Yale and Princeton to New York City, and the fact that Hobey Baker was playing, their hockey match of 1913 was carefully chronicled by the *New York Times*. There is ample evidence of Baker's singular dominance: he was credited with 30 of Princeton's 42 shots. The *Times* correspondent couldn't help but gush over Baker. "Hobey, the spectacular rover, was all over the rink, skimming up and down the ice like a shadow. He was going so fast that the Yale players went down before him." And in their overtime period, Baker scored an unforgettable goal. "He started as dazzling an exhibition of skating as had ever been seen on the rink, a series of zig-zag dashes…carried the puck to every part of the ice surface without being touched and brought the game to a thrilling finish." [14] Dominating games so thoroughly, all under the spotlight of heavyweight newspapers between Boston and New York, blew up Baker's fame to unfathomable heights.

Yet sportsmanship continued to be of paramount importance to Hobey, even more so than winning. His response to being fouled by dreaded "muckers" crushed him emotionally. During one game, Hobey was illegally hauled to the ice after he got behind the enemy defenders, causing a major meltdown. In the subsequent intermission, Hobey was found crying into his hands in the locker room.

"Forget it Hobe, we still have another chance at them," said a teammate.

"It's not the game," said Hobey, looking up, his face wet with tears. "To think that a *friend* would do such a thing!" [15]

As his career continued, Hobey had no choice but to develop a thicker skin, especially against players outside his circle of familiar prep rivals. Princeton played semipro teams from both sides of the border that knew the key to victory against the Tigers boiled down to a simple game plan—"Get Baker." Every opponent embraced the doctrine as soon as they saw Hobey's name over the entrance to the arena. Opponents, particularly those without prep school pedigrees, were determined to neutralize Baker by any means necessary: hook, trip, butt end. But every account reveals Baker being unfazed by the thuggery, bouncing up enthusiastically from each of the various muggings.

It was in college that he began a tradition of visiting the enemy locker room to shake hands with all his opponents, clean or dirty, often the same men who had just assaulted him on the ice. Hobey's penchant for post-game handshakes may have been the first recognized act of what is now a sacred hockey tradition.

After being brutalized on the ice, Hobey's idea of retaliation was to score another goal. Although no official records were kept, biographer Salvini used newspaper accounts to peg Hobey's career scoring mark at 120 goals. That is nearly twice as many as Princeton's official career goal scoring king John Cook (Class of 1963), who totaled 67 over his three-year career. Unofficially, Hobey averaged a hat trick (three goals) per game as a collegian, so it is no wonder teams would employ desperate methods to try and stop him.

No one prepared for Hobey more than Harvard, due to the efforts of their Hall-of-Fame coach Alfred Winsor, a tireless tactician. His Crimson squad was Hobey's foil in the greatest game of his college career. No one lucky enough to score a ticket to the Princeton-Harvard game on January 24, 1914, ever forgot it. This was the night Hobey became a true icon in the hub of eastern hockey—Boston.

There was a huge buzz prior to this matchup of college hockey's superpowers. Scalpers on Huntington Avenue conducted brisk business prior to the Saturday afternoon sellout at Boston Arena. According to biographer Davies, there was "a good deal of betting," on this game, with the Tigers established as 10-7 favorites by the bookmakers. [16] By 1914, Harvard was building its own hockey legacy, and they were determined to slow, if not stop, the irresistible force that was Hobey Baker. Now a senior who had just celebrated his 22nd birthday, Baker received a standing ovation from the hockey-savvy crowd when he stepped onto the ice, the atmosphere electric.

It was another historical figure, however, who stole the show this night. Massachusetts political giant Leverett Saltonstall played only briefly in that storied match, but he will forever be associated with its lore. Fifty years after that contest, 69-year-old Senator Saltonstall wrote about the game as if he had just stepped off the sheet. "When Baker started up the ice, the crowd always either rose or became tremendously excited and screamed—'Here he comes!'" said Saltonstall. [17] Harvard was not intimidated by the aura of superstar Hobey Baker: they had beaten Princeton two out of three times the previous season to wrest the intercollegiate championship from the Tigers.

Substitute Saltonstall may have been a terrific rower for Harvard, but he was a sluggish skater, relegated to the role of benchwarmer for the speedy Crimson hockey clubs. He analyzed this classic game from memories gleaned mostly from the spectators' side of the boards.

"When Hobey took the puck from behind his own goal, he used to zig-zag and dribble up the rink without looking at the puck," said Saltonstall. "[Coach] Winsor taught us to keep our lanes and come back as fast as we could so that we would not give him an opening to jump between us." [18] Although Harvard managed to keep Hobey off the scoreboard this night, it was more a result of the marvelous skills of Crimson goaltender Guvvy Carnochan than any clever coaching.

Baker and Kuhn were superb through regulation, and Hobey's wingman snuck one past Carnochan from the left side to open the scoring 15 minutes into the contest. Crimson sniper Morgan Phillips answered moments later, splitting the Princeton defense in a spectacular individual effort, causing the rafters to shudder from the fans' raucous response. Those two goals, less than a minute apart, represented the only scoring in 90 minutes of scintillating hockey, a marathon of a game much like the televised NCAA championship overtime thrillers that followed later in the century.

Not that there wasn't action from this game suitable for a time capsule: Princeton poured 36 shots on Carnochan, who used all his body parts to repel the identified flying objects. Hobey, who "seemed to be everywhere on the ice," had two glorious chances to put the Crimson away with breakaways, indelible moments that brought Boston's faithful out of their seats, hearts in their throats. On the first, he fired a quick wrist shot that was coolly turned aside by Carnochan; on the second, Harvard's defenseman Bill Claflin hauled him down from behind. Penalty shots were not awarded back in the day. "Bill was put off the ice for two minutes," said Saltonstall, "but the game was saved." [19]

After 40 minutes of regulation, and another 10 of scheduled overtime, the two captains—Kuhn and Harvard's Bill Willets— were summoned to center ice. They agreed to play sudden death hockey until the game was decided, one way or another, even if it took all night. The Boston crowd roared with approval, and most remained standing the rest of the way.

It became a war of attrition, as several exhausted Harvard forwards asked to be taken out. It was reported that players lost an average of four pounds of water weight in this game, Carnochan nine. The machine-like Hobey reportedly, "wasn't even breathing hard." [20]

At the game's 80-minute mark, Crimson coach Winsor saw his second-to-last forward beg out of the game. He looked down the bench and gave a quick nod to the lumbering Saltonstall. Despite being the freshest skater in the building, he was still out of his league. "Even at that point I could not skate as fast as Baker or some of the others," said the future governor and senator from Massachusetts. Ten minutes later, destiny called.

"Paul Smart [Harvard] took the puck down the rink," recalled Saltonstall, "hit the defense, and the puck went up in the air and came down at my feet as I was thundering along." Saltonstall's use of the verb "thundering" may have been an embellishment. He did, however, find himself with a world of opportunity. "There was nothing between me and the goal. I made the quick decision that I would be better off to try and shoot than to try and fool him and dribble the puck in." So Saltonstall launched the puck, a changeup of sorts that made time stand still, all eyes on the black disc as it floated past players' shoulders on its way toward the Princeton net. Tigers' goalie Frank Winants waived at the puck prematurely, and it bounced into the goal, touching off a celebration for the ages. Saltonstall, however, was subdued in his recollection: "I was lucky enough to break the tie." [21]

Bedlam reigned from ice level to the far reaches of the Boston Arena balconies. Delirious fans who had paid four times face value for their ticket knew they had just experienced the sports bargain of a lifetime. Harvard's forgotten man, stapled to the end of the bench, had miraculously conquered Hobey Baker's Princeton Tigers. The headlines from this historic game would be outlasted by its oral history, which began immediately in the excited taverns of Copley Square, Back Bay, and within the dorms of Harvard Yard. The Crimson had beaten the legendary Hobey Baker in the greatest game of all time.

The post script to that spectacle was that Princeton came back to beat Harvard twice more that season, giving Hobey's Tigers their second national championship in his three years of college hockey. Nevertheless, Senator Saltonstall cherished his moment of hockey immortality, calling it the greatest thrill of his life, beyond that of his many accomplishments in the political arena. He gave his stick divine status, the *Excalibur* that smote Hobey Baker. He brought it out only to teach his grandchildren hockey out on the frozen ponds of suburban Boston, and used it as a prop when he shared the story of how together, they had beaten the great Hobey Baker.

Hobey still had some history of his own to achieve, and even added to his lore as an endurance monster before his college career was over. Following the championship game rematch against Harvard—a 4-1 win at Saint Nicholas Arena in which Baker set up three of the Tiger goals—Hobey learned that Fellowes and the wildcat McMahon brothers had arranged a challenge match with St. Nick's the next day, one that would bring yet another chorus of paying customers into the big house. The only problem was, several members of the Princeton squad had grabbed the first train home that morning, and the Tigers only had six players remaining, one fewer than a starting lineup. But Baker and Kuhn were having too much fun to quit just yet, so they agreed to play a man short. St. Nick's was eager to take on Baker and Company: they were seasoned, fresh, and had bodies to spare. The Tigers skeleton crew extended their season by clawing out one last home victory, 2-1 over the frustrated St. Nick's squad. Hobey and his five mates were completely spent, when, incredibly, the St. Nick's management came knocking once again.

Cornelius Fellowes had found one final opponent, and for the promoters, another payday. They weren't sure if and when their marvelous meal-ticket Hobey Baker would play again in their venue, so they set up another match, this time with the U.S. Army 7th Regiment, who had come down from nearby West Point. Barely an hour had passed since Princeton's grueling game with St. Nick's.

The response from Hobey and company was predictable: *Why not?* Another group of fans paid their way and scaled the stairs into the Saint Nick's balcony for a final glimpse of Baker in Tiger stripes. He did not disappoint, leading Princeton to a remarkable 4-0 win over the crestfallen cadets. Baker concluded his otherworldly college career at Saint Nicholas Arena with three sizeable victories in just 26 hours: a college championship game, a shorthanded win over the men of St. Nick's, and a shutout finale over fresh military cadets [22] Fellowes and the McMahon brothers had maximized every ounce of Hobey's energy, converting his efforts into gold for their coffers, yet Baker never blinked.

Despite being a New York hockey treasure, the rest of the country could not help but appreciate Baker's other-worldly gifts on the ice. The *Boston Journal* published a story stating that Hobey was "Without a doubt the greatest hockey player ever developed in this country or Canada." [23] America's weary legend finally got on the train home to Princeton, heading back for a long, and much deserved, sleep.

The next weekend, another hockey road trip beckoned. Canada wanted one more Hobey experience, this time up in the nation's capital for an exhibition against Ottawa's best amateur club. Hobey was treated as visiting hockey royalty. Keep in mind that Canada, then as today, has rarely considered Americans as anything other than second-class hockey citizens. But Hobey was an exception. After a couple of "friendly" exhibitions, the hosts pulled out all the stops for a first-class formal dinner. That night Baker was officially crowned "The King of Hockey" by Ottawa's lords of sport. Elated by such an honor, it is reported that Hobey imbibed hard alcohol for the first time that night, sampling a scotch and soda after his final college game. [24] Hobey had ample reason to celebrate: for Canada to honor an American as the king of their national sport is something that had never happened before, nor since.

HOBEYQUEST: FINDING EXCALIBUR

Ron Fimrite's enthralling article on Hobey Baker in the March 19, 1991 issue of Sports Illustrated did a great deal to return Hobey, deceased for over 70 years at the time of its publishing, to the sporting mainstream.

As an independent TV producer fascinated with Hobey's legend, I often returned to the Fimrite story on-line. It was during one of those visits that an electronic letter to the editor jumped off the screen. Richard Byrd, one of Leverett Saltonstall's grandchildren and another Harvard hockey man, had written in. In his letter, Byrd described how Gramps used to take him out on the frozen ponds to teach him hockey, and how he wore the same skates and used the same stick that had defeated the great Hobey Baker. In the closing paragraph, Byrd mentioned that the stick had been bequeathed to the Harvard hockey office. As a faculty brat who grew up in Cambridge, I knew my way around the red brick campus; I paused and made a vigorous mental note.

Days later, I was up in Cambridge visiting family and invited the high-octane Bill Cleary to help me search the Harvard athletic offices. He just so happened to be coming up from Cape Cod that day, so he agreed to meet me outside the Dillon Field House, the former home of the Harvard hockey office. Although he had retired as athletic director over a decade prior, the gregarious Cleary was completely at home inside the Crimson sports complex, remembering everyone's name—from maintenance men, to secretaries, to athletic trainers. He procured a key in short order, and we soon found ourselves in Coach Ted Donato's old office,

Harvard hockey legend Bill Cleary holding the stick that struck the winning blow for the Crimson, beating Hobey's Princeton Tigers in 1914. This contest was long known as the greatest college game of all time. (Tim Rappleye)

creeping in like a couple of cat burglars. The spacious room glowed from a fresh coat of white paint; despite the blinds being drawn, there was ample light.

Fifteen feet from the desk was the hockey closet, not unlike an unkempt locker stall, except that it was closed off by a door. It was tall, and had two levels. Cleary was in charge and thoroughly enjoying himself, pulling out old jerseys and commemorative pucks. Then he got excited and beckoned me over. He pulled out a hockey stick whose blade was fully wrapped with black friction tape. Once I saw "Northland Pro" on the shaft, I lost some of my buzz; this stick was far too modern to be from Hobey's era. Cleary, on the other hand, was getting red in the face, all pumped up. He extended the stick in front of him, as if posing for a hockey promotional video.

"This is my stick from Squaw Valley!" said Cleary, jabbing the air with his old wand. It was clear that the leading scorer from the 1960 Olympics was poised to light the lamp once again, with the same twig, no less. As a onetime chronicler of Team USA's gold medal run at the 1960 Winter Games, my mood swung back to positive. Cleary's enthusiasm was indeed infectious.

Then he redirected his famous energy back to the task, thrashing about in the closet's distant corners. Moments later he emerged with what looked like a narrow, brown branch. It…was…an…antique hockey stick! We laughed in joyful unison, feeling like Howard Carter in King Tut's tomb. There it was, Excalibur itself, the sword that smote Hobey Baker a century prior. I grasped it and held it carefully, feeling hockey history traveling up and down my arms. Cleary was beaming his signature victory smile, revealing a mouth full of gold-laden teeth. This was a pretty cool dream: a couple of hockey maniacs from Cambridge locked away in the Harvard hockey office, unearthing two immortal hockey sticks.

Then I looked down the ancient shaft to the blade, and something caught my eye. Engraved into the heel of the stick was the word "Brine," with a branded circle around it; the flip side had an identical mark. Holy Moly! Brine was still a major player in New England sporting goods. There was no doubt in my mind that not only had we found the ultimate artifact, but it included a sponsor for the next Hobey video project. What an unbelievable morning we were sharing!

There has always been magical energy surrounding Cleary, and that day it manifested itself once again. Closing century-long gaps to flesh out Hobey Baker history is both challenging and frustrating; so many of my chases had been of the "wild goose" variety. But on that particular Thursday in Cambridge, the other King of American Hockey made the process both fun and easy, with a virtual stop in Squaw Valley thrown in for good measure.

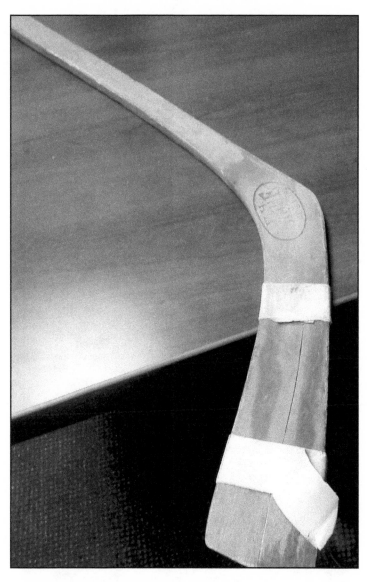

*This ancient hockey stick belonged to Harvard player Leverett
Salsonstall. The future U.S. Senator from Massachusetts
used this stick to defeat Hobey's championship squad from
Princeton in triple overtime. (Tim Rappleye)*

Although the lightest football player at Princeton, Baker blossomed into a star, leading the Tigers to a national championship and being named to two All-America teams. In 1975 Hobey was inducted into the College Football Hall of Fame. (Getty Images)

CHAPTER FIVE

Biggest Man on Campus

P hiladelphia was no place for Hobey in the summer of 1912. Family life, at least the version he liked to recall, had been uprooted. Hobey's mom was lost to historians, presumed to be in an institution. Meanwhile, his father was described as being confined to a wheelchair, his motor skills steadily deteriorating. The "infirm" 49-year-old Bobby Baker had remarried and was living with the family of Laura Butcher in downtown Philadelphia. Rather than thrust himself into those decidedly uncomfortable surroundings, Hobey accepted the invitation to visit the sandy shores of Manchester, Massachusetts, and hang out with a couple of his former St. Paul's buddies.

Always stoked for action, these boys of privilege had access to a Simplex race car, a German-made Mercedes that had become popular with wealthy sportsmen because it was winning high-profile races throughout the U.S. It had neither a windshield nor a back seat, but it did have room for a driver and passenger on a plush leather bench behind a large steering wheel, as well as generous running boards on either side. The owner of the car and his brother occupied the seats in the cab, while Hobey jumped on the side, holding onto the passenger door for dear life. The driver cranked up the powerful Simplex engine, the tachometer needle jumped, and they began their joy-ride down the Yankee Division Highway, a mile inland from the Atlantic Ocean. Twenty-year old Hobey was having the time of his life; he felt entirely secure with both hands on the passenger door and feet planted. He hung out over the road, enjoying the wind rushing through his blond hair. Hobey whooped during each high-speed turn, balancing on the edge of the car like the sailors racing in the Atlantic a mile away.

They suddenly veered off Yankee Highway onto a narrow dirt road, trying to maintain their speed over the rough terrain. Each bump generated shrieks from the thrilled riders. The driver accelerated into a blind turn, and then gulped at what he saw. The boys found themselves heading toward an equally fast oncoming car, the joy ride now one of sheer terror. Hobey's driver slammed on the brakes and yanked the steering wheel to the left, avoiding the head-on collision, but effectively launching Baker from the running board. He sailed through the air like a high diver, heading toward a wooden fence. The two brothers stared in amazement as Hobey reacted in mid-air, curling his body so that his shoulder, not his head, hit the fence gate. He rolled as he dropped to the ground, lightly returned to his feet, and trotted back to the car. The driver was dumbfounded. "Why he wasn't killed, I don't know," said Hobey's companion. "That was one of the most amazing athletic feats I've ever seen in my life. I know darn well he must have known what he was doing. He was absolutely fearless." [1]

With his family life in tatters, what threat was physical harm to Hobey? Conquering risk of bodily destruction was Hobey's escape from emotional pain and doubt. When he returned to campus that fall, halfway through his college career, Hobey Baker was a perfect physical specimen. Although quickly becoming the most admired man on campus, he harbored a host of disquieting secrets. His supreme athleticism helped shield him from those doubts. Baker's outrageous feats, never before seen on sports' grandest venues, made him a young immortal. When taking his daily walks from the Ivy dining club to classes at Nassau Hall, Hobey was insulated from any gossip or the prying of strangers. As a high-profile sports deity, his status was unimpeachable—Hobey was Princeton's biggest man on campus.

It was during his junior year when Hobey found his stride in football. He added a wrinkle to his punt returning that nearly revolutionized the sport. He learned to precisely judge the landing spot of the punts he was about to receive, and would then line up five yards *behind* that projected point. With the enemy's punt coverage team closing in to punish him, at the last possible moment Hobey would sprint five yards past them, field the punt at full speed, and leave his pursuers in the dust, literally. It gave him ample space to ignite his open field runs at full throttle, reading and reacting in hyperspeed as he weaved towards the goal line, acquiring gobs of yardage for the Tigers.

On autumn Saturdays, Baker was a 60-minute man. In addition to being a stalwart running back on offense, and a special teams demon, returning punts and racking up points as a dropkicker, Hobey was also the last line of defense as the Tigers' deep safety. He was the Tigers swiftest defender and surest tackler.

Instead of three or four thousand hockey fans thrilling to Hobey, it was now ten times that number in the Eastern football coliseums. Both high society and common man flocked to see Baker the football hero, and he never disappointed. There are newspaper accounts of his 85-yard punt return versus Dartmouth that are beyond belief, with all of his twists and turns, his frequent reversing of direction before ultimately finding the end zone. New Jersey Governor and presidential candidate Woodrow Wilson wedged himself into University Field at the Dartmouth game, delighting in Hobey's wizardry along with rest of Tiger football nation. Incredibly, Baker topped that feat with another mind-bender before the season was out. In the 1912 finale versus Yale, he returned a punt 88 yards for a TD in front of his adoring throng. Princeton football fans were experiencing the Hobey rush every Saturday home game for three years running.

Throughout his career, Baker fielded over 20 punts per game on average, frequently with the game on the line because of the low-scoring nature of Eastern football. Hobey was money in the bank, the most sure-handed returner in the land. Fans didn't need to master the nuances of football to experience Baker's greatness, they simply located the shock of blonde hair and followed the flight of the punt; it was at their intersection where the adventure began.

The thrills were two-sided: Hobey's brain was marinating in adrenaline and endorphins during the punt returns that sent fans into their delirium. Every opposing punt was an opportunity for the blonde, unhelmeted Baker to showcase his dynamic skill set: stops, starts, even backwards running to avoid a smashing tackle. His brain was taking in 360 degrees of swirling data, all while players in foreign colors closed in with deadly intent. Exuberant biographer Emil Salvini calculated that Baker fielded 900 career punts and averaged 300 yards per game on punt returns in his three varsity seasons. Salvini's estimate is significantly higher than fellow biographer Davies, who claimed that Hobey averaged 180 yards per game fielding punts. One fact is irrefutable: the majority of the offensive yardage Princeton gained during the Hobey Baker era was generated by his punt returns, not from the line of scrimmage. Hobey Baker was indeed, *The Show.*

On the first Tuesday in November, 1912, New Jersey Governor Woodrow Wilson was restless, and wanted to stretch his legs; he decided to take an afternoon stroll. He exited his tony three-story Tudor on Cleveland Lane and headed southeast towards University Field. It was election day, and Wilson's name was at the top of the Democratic ticket, taking on the Republican incumbent William Howard Taft as well as former president Teddy Roosevelt, representing the short-lived Bull Moose party. The new telephone that Wilson thought was so wonderful a couple years earlier was now becoming a menace. Pesky reporters had that contraption ringing non-stop since Wilson returned from the Democratic Convention in July, so he decided to de-stress by going across town to watch Princeton's football practice.

It took the 5'11" Wilson around 20 minutes before he was seated at the edge of the grandstand. It was cool and cloudy, but there was no rain in sight. He was soon chatting tactics with Princeton's designated annual coach Logan Cunningham. Wilson, like President Nixon 60 years later, loved to kibitz about gridiron tactics and draw plays on napkins. Unlike Nixon, Wilson was a real football man, having coached at Wesleyan for two years prior to returning to Princeton as its president in 1902. As an undergraduate, Wilson was the secretary of the Princeton Football Association when they won the 1878 national championship. Known as a creative innovator while at Wesleyan, Wilson knew college football's intricacies better than Cunningham.

This was Wilson's third visit to a Tigers' practice that season. [2] Like so many others, he was enamored with the undersized blonde fellow on the far side of the field, tirelessly shagging punts. He and Cunningham discussed Princeton's loss to undefeated Harvard the week before, and their prospects for beating Yale in ten days. Then Wilson let Cunningham return to his tasks, and stretched out on the spectator benches in rare solitude. He loved watching Baker go about his routines, drop-kicking field goals from every white stripe on the field. Wilson tried to imagine what it must feel like to be both so physically brilliant and such a popular hero to the Princeton community. He smiled, stood up, and brushed the wrinkles from his suit before pacing home to 25 Cleveland Lane. That evening Wilson learned that he was the president-elect of the United States. He and his wife Ellen began planning the move from his beloved Princeton to Washington D.C.

In 1912, Hobey's junior year, Princeton outplayed Yale in their finale, but were forced to settle for a 6-6 tie, completing their season with a 7-1-1 record. Hobey was now a college football treasure, dazzling every fan who came to see him play. Baker shared the philosophy of "The Great One," Wayne Gretzky— never have an off-day because that game might be the only one some fan might get to see you play. The *Boston Herald* spoke for the country when it claimed, "Hobe[y] Baker is the most feared open field runner playing football. Let him get free and clear and it is 'good night' to the pursuers." [3]

Baker seemed to balance every magnificent highlight with a comparable act of sportsmanship. Dartmouth's All-American defensive end Red Louden was once knocked unconscious in an unsuccessful attempt to tackle Hobey. He only learned after the fact that he was carried off the field by the Princeton star. Louden kept the newspaper clip documenting Baker's selfless act in his wallet for years afterward. [4]

Princeton ceded their national championship crown to undefeated Harvard in 1912, as Yale, Princeton and upstart Carlisle all finished with a solitary loss. In the all-American voting, Jim Thorpe and Baker joined Harvard's Charles Brickley as the nation's top halfbacks. It is a pity that America's two supreme athletes, Baker and Thorpe, never faced each other on the gridiron. Incredibly, Thorpe had dominated the 1912 Olympics that previous summer, winning both the Pentathlon and the Decathlon in Stockholm, before returning to the Carlisle campus that fall. One can only speculate how the Native American would have fared on a pair of ice skates.

From all accounts, Baker spent most of his college life either training or studying. There are no reports of a steady girlfriend or any women in particular that caught his eye. When it came to the typical adolescent skirt-chasing, roommate Wen Kuhn spoke for Hobey. "I don't think it interested him much in school or college." [5] Baker may have been too prim and proper to parlay his sporting fame into a romantic liaison. During a hockey intermission up in Boston, Hobey was invited on a double-date by a pair of bachelorettes after the contest. Their note was delivered on scented paper to the locker room, within it a promise to have a limo parked in front of the Boston Arena for a post-game rendezvous. The girls lived up to their end of the bargain, but the prudish Baker was "petrified," and was led out of the back of the Arena through the boiler room exit. [6] He may have had no qualms risking his neck defying gravity and angry pursuers, but when it came to fast women, Hobey was scared stiff.

After consuming a single beer, however, Baker's inhibitions would melt away. According to roommate Emmons, "On one glass of beer, he would be just as high as he would be on two-dozen." [7] It can be safely assumed that Hobey had quaffed at least one beer the night he streaked—naked as the proverbial jaybird—from Princeton's Holder Hall to the cannons in front of Nassau Hall, under the chilly moonlight. The total distance of his roundtrip foray was three lengths of a football field, and Hobey won his bet. [8] There was no report of him being at all winded after his birthday-suit sprint.

Hobey's silliness sparked by a glass of beer or champagne often triggered a reckless streak as well. A fellow Ivy Club member recalls a night in Manhattan at the Plaza, where the fellows convened for a bachelor dinner. After helping himself to a glass of the bubbly (or two), Hobey led a group of post-adolescents in black tie out for some fresh air, through the French windows onto a narrow ledge, *high above Central Park South.* [9] As said so many times, the man was fearless, if not wise.

Based on several anecdotes and the fact that Hobey resisted wearing any kind of headgear in either football or hockey, Baker has been deemed "narcissistic" by Davies and his fellow biographers. There are several stories that support that claim, like the evening before a freshman baseball challenge against the Princeton sophomores. Hobey spent much of that night in his apartment trying to perfect the ideal hook slide into a pillow, over and over, never quite content with the result. He repeatedly analyzed his precise execution, captivated by his own body's movement.

Hobey's physique was his glorious tool, the vehicle that helped him maintain unquestioned status on a campus full of society swells, the trump card that kept his insecurities at bay. It served another purpose, as well. Hobey's body was his thrill machine. When he got it cranked up, especially in the heat of athletic battle, it gave him adrenaline rushes that mere mortals could only obtain illegally. And there was a third consequence to owning such a heavenly body, a condensed version of Michelangelo's David: it generated powerful hormonal responses from all observers, men and women.

Henry Beyer was a classmate who remembered Hobey vividly. "I could still visualize that amazing Greek God physique, the finest, I believe, I have ever seen," said Beyer, who was married with three children while writing this recollection. "It was difficult to take my eyes off that wonderful, beautiful body." [10]

W.T. Shackleford was only slightly less effusive. "He was one of the most handsome youngsters I ever saw in my life, the glamor boy of campus." Shackleford then included a crucial addendum. "None of which went to his head." [11] Hobey's senior year roommate Rolf Bauhan wrote about Hobey's reluctance to bring any attention to himself. "He was self-effacing to a fault, he hated publicity," said Bauhan. "I remember his hiding when press photographers and reporters wanted to interview him." [12]

Donald "Heff" Herring was Hobey's academic counselor and assistant football coach, and he was tuned into his young charge's Odylic force. "Hobey was the type of male animal that attracts women, of all classes, by a look, or a nod of the head." [13]

Herring, seemingly omnipresent in both Hobey's life and death, knew the young man better than any Princetonian. He described Hobey as also having a good sense of humor. "He had a low chuckle, and a faint smile at the corner of his mouth...an inner amusement he may or may not share with you." Herring put extra emphasis on his final description of Baker. "Hobey despised pomposity." [14] Of the countless depictions and platitudes directed toward Hobey while at Princeton, his humility may have been the most prevalent. For all of his popularity and irresistible attraction, Hobey was not stuck up. He may have been shy, and was clearly not gregarious, but on and off the playing fields, Hobey was kind and selfless.

He was also tender. During one summer break while at St. Paul's, Hobey worked as a camp counselor for boys out in the Catskills mountain range in upstate New York. Hobey stayed in touch with a young fellow named Underhill, and years later invited him to Princeton to take in a home football game, knowing it might be a thrill for the lad. The game turned out to be a crushing loss to Harvard, a contest decided by a buzzer-beating drop kick from Hobey's chief Crimson rival Charles Brickley. Forty years later Underhill recalled tears in Hobey's eyes when they reconvened after the game. [15]

It is often said that the best way to judge a man's character is by how he treats his subordinates, individuals from whom he has nothing to gain. Hazing freshmen was a ritualized sport during Hobey's time at Princeton; first-year students were easy targets with their embarrassing little beanie hats. One grateful member of the class of 1915 recalled Hobey showing rare mercy. "We were harassed by a singularly bad group of horses' asses in Hobey's class," recalled the alum. "But along came Hobey with a smile and always courteous. What a relief to meet a sophomore who was a gentleman and did not degrade himself to take advantage of poor kids who couldn't talk back." [16]

Both Davies and *Sports Illustrated's* Ron Fimrite shared a story demonstrating how sensitive Hobey was to others' feelings. At graduation, classmate J. Henry O'Neill, clearly in awe of the god-like Baker, was giving his parents a tour of the campus when Hobey sped by on his bicycle. The boy summoned up the courage to shout out a quick hello, which prompted Hobey to skid to a stop, disembark and jog back with a smile, "Gee, I was afraid you weren't going to stop me," said Hobey, who visited briefly with the elated O'Neill and his family. [17]

Baker had another wide-eyed admirer at Princeton, a mere freshman during Baker's senior year. The impressionable teenager was F. Scott Fitzgerald, and he too was the beneficiary of Hobey's kindness. Fitzgerald spent much his life smitten by Hobey's character, describing him as "an ideal worthy of everything in my enthusiastic admiration, yet consummated and expressed in a human being who stood within ten feet of me." [18] Fitzgerald included two variations of Baker in his first novel, *This Side of Paradise*. He transposed Hobey's middle name onto his protagonist—Amory Blaine. In addition, Hobey himself has an unmistakable role in the book as the character Allenby, Princeton's football immortal.

> *There at the head of the white platoon marched Allenby, the football captain, slim and defiant, as if aware that this year the hopes of the college rested on him, that his hundred and sixty pounds were expected to dodge to victory through the heavy blue and crimson lines.* [19]

Fitzgerald fantasized about being a Princeton gridiron hero himself, going so far as to have his mom ship him a set of football pads shortly after he arrived on campus. But the spindly Fitzgerald quickly flamed out on the freshman squad, and his dream remained just that.

Football worship was the anchor of a rigid Ivy League class system that so dominated early 20th century college life. Similarly, gaining membership to the exclusive dining clubs was also vital to students desperate to find their place in the social hierarchy. It is no wonder how much Ivy league hero worship colored the characters in Fitzgerald's writing, from Amory Blaine in *This Side of Paradise* to Tom Buchanan in *The Great Gatsby*.

English professor Anne Margaret Daniel, the pre-eminent authority on all things Fitzgerald, said that his gaining membership into one of Princeton's dining clubs was one of the most gratifying accomplishments in his abbreviated college career. "Fitzgerald *loved* being a member of the Cottage Club," said Daniel. Although a non-entity in the Ivy League sports world, Fitzgerald wrote from experience about the sacred dining clubs that line Prospect Avenue in Princeton:

> *Ivy, detached and breathlessly aristocratic; Cottage, an impressive mélange of brilliant adventurers and well-dressed philanderers; Tiger Inn, broad-shouldered and athletic, vitalized by an honest elaboration of prep school standards; Cap and Gown, anti-alcoholic, faintly religious and politically powerful.* [20]

Due to Hobey's lineage and unparalleled stardom on the playing fields, he was instantly whisked into Ivy, Princeton's most exclusive club, as a matter of course. Football was social currency at Princeton, and Hobey was a walking Fort Knox.

Football season drove every student at Princeton (and Harvard and Yale) a little bonkers with anticipation, especially prior to a game against one of the Big Three. There was little focus in the classroom, and rarely full attendance. Davies wrote from personal experience about football mania at Ol' Nassau before big games: torch-lit parades, former legends coming back to campus to re-enact winning plays of yore, and tales of amped up gangs of 20-year-olds whose college spirit often spilled over. Davies referred to it simply as "civic religion." It was within that autumn mania that classmate William Tippetts was blown away by Hobey's unfathomable cool. "The morning of an important Yale game he attended class, nonchalant and calm," writes Tippetts. "No one would have known from the way he talked and acted that he was to play that afternoon." [21]

With Hobey leading by conscientious example, the football Tigers finished at 5-2-1 his senior year, losing to powerful Harvard and nearly drowning in a rain-soaked 6-0 loss to Dartmouth. New Haven was the setting for Hobey's final act as a football player, one that salvaged their season. The *New York Times* devoted ample space in November 1913 as to how Baker preserved a tie with Yale in the last minute of the game. He found himself chasing down the Eli's star running back Forester Ainesworth for 84 long yards, the game's outcome hanging in the balance. "One by one, he (Ainesworth) passed the Princeton tacklers, now free and clear of everybody but Hobey Baker. The Princeton captain alone could save Princeton now." [22] With every fan at Yale Field clutching their chest, Hobey calmly stalked his prey, waiting until the last possible moment before pouncing, de-cleating Ainesworth at the Princeton six yard line. In one of his final acts on the gridiron, Hobey crushed the Eli dreams, keeping intact his career record of never losing to Yale.

And thus concluded Hobey Baker's football career. He returned to the Walter Camp All-America Team as the number three ranked halfback of 1913, his second appearance on that prestigious list. He had come to Princeton from St. Paul's, where hockey reigned supreme and football was merely an afterthought. Princeton, on the other hand, worshipped football and was a national contender against powerhouses Yale and Harvard. Hobey, the lightest man in the program, willed himself into stardom in the country's most popular sport, at its highest level. His accolades and accomplishments in football were considerable: a national championship, a two-time All-American, a team captain, and the holder of Princeton's single-season scoring record for 62 years. In 1975 Hobey Baker was elected to the College Football Hall of Fame. All this from a man who considered football his second sport.

Contrary to the opinions of hero-worshipers like F. Scott Fitzgerald, Hobey's role on campus was much more than that of mere superjock. Thanks to the efforts of former Princeton president Woodrow Wilson, Hobey's academic life was thoroughly intertwined with his "preceptor," a counselor/teacher who worked closely with a small group of students. A preceptor was intended to inspire these young men of privilege to embrace learning for learning's sake. Prior to Wilson introducing the program in 1905, Princeton had earned a reputation as a country club for the old boy network. Wilson borrowed the "preceptor" concept from the Oxford system of engaged teaching. He wanted to end the era of lectures and readings by detached professors, which was essentially an extension of prep school.

Hobey's preceptor was Heff Herring, not only a former Princeton football player but a Rhodes Scholar as well—giving him first-hand knowledge of the Oxford system. Mentor and protégé first teamed up during Hobey's junior year, forming a partnership of mutual admiration both on the football field and in the classroom. Herring pushed Hobey in the classics, insisting on the same kind of effort he saw every fall afternoon at practice. The loyal Hobey repeatedly met the challenge, in one instance reading 50,000 words in preparation for a paper on Queen Elizabeth's Spanish policy. [23] Like nearly all his grades at Princeton, Hobey got a 'B' on the paper.

Classmate James MacColl was not terribly impressed with Hobey's intellect, but admired his determination. "He was only a fair student, who had to work extremely hard to attain a good standing," wrote MacColl years later. "When the rest of the boys were playing cards or other games, Hobey was always studying." [24] Baker had neither the time nor the intellectual curiosity to be an 'A' student, but he never shirked his studies, always faithful to Herring's demands. As was Wilson's intent, the preceptor and the student, seven years apart in age, became true friends.

To many, the beautiful and reticent Baker was simply impossible to approach. Sometimes, it required the help of Princeton's alphabetical classroom seating for an ordinary fellow to get his attention. During his freshman year, Hobey was seated next to awestruck Henry Beyer in German class. "I was a scholarship boy, slated to wait on tables for four years, and there was the great Hobey Baker!" Beyer went on to describe how Hobey actually paid a visit to his room, and asked him to return to the Sweet Pea to study together. This was an offer to which Beyer most enthusiastically complied. [25]

Beyer was fascinated by Baker at college, recalling his careful observations four decades after their time together on campus. "He used to take puffs of classmates' cigarettes," said Beyer with incredulity, "even during the height of the football season. I saw him do it a number of times!" It was as if Beyer had spied Santa Claus nipping from a flask. In Beyer's mind, it humanized Hobey, which broadened his love for him. "He was the finest boy who ever stepped on the Princeton campus. His untimely passing still saddens me." [26]

Another alphabetical classroom neighbor wasn't quite so enamored by Hobey's distant cool. Paxton Blair, a future New York State supreme court justice, spent an entire semester seated next to the detached superstar. Baker must have spent the duration without volunteering a word to the prickly Blair, who fired this note off to Davies: "Hobey Baker was an unconscionable and ill-mannered snob." [27]

Despite not being a man of the people, Baker was named captain of the hockey team his junior year, and captain of the football team his senior year. Davies queried several teammates about Hobey's captain qualities, and they portrayed Hobey as atypical. "He was too much the loner," concluded Davies. "Too aloof to slap rumps, reprimand the lazy, keep up the constant flow of chatter which the duties of captain call for." [28]

The portrait of Hobey's life at Ol Nassau would not be complete without mentioning his love of singing. The purity of the notes emanating from his diaphragm reflected Hobey's simple beauty. He never missed an opportunity to express himself in song: in the locker room, on the steps of Nassau Hall, or on formal road trips as a member of Princeton's Glee Club double quartet. And when he wasn't singing, he was often heard humming; the man always seemed to be accompanied by song. Classmate Beyer recalled in awe how Hobey could wedge a pencil between his teeth to create a makeshift instrument to play "Alexander's Ragtime Band." [29] Later in life, Baker often traveled with his trusty ukulele for accompaniment. His voice continued its march down the octaves as he aged—no longer the Saint Paul's alto, he was first bass at Princeton. Davies lists Hobey's favorite tunes: "Moonlight Bay," "Roll Dem Bones," "Sweet Adeline," and "Honolulu Tomboy." [30] His lyrical expression was emblematic of Hobey's giving nature: he loved to perform and bring joy to his audience, big or small.

Hobey lived his life in frequent conflict between his need for individual expression and his disdain for showoffs. This anomaly was evident every time Hobey would be hunted down for a quote by a breathless reporter following yet another supreme performance on the ice or the gridiron. "You would oblige me by saying nothing at all," was the typical Hobey response [31] Classmate Rolf Bauhan described how Hobey often hid from photographers and reporters after big games. Baker may have hated publicity, but he couldn't help himself from generating it. This paradoxical push and pull tormented Baker most of his life.

Hobey crammed a lifetime of athletic achievement into a four-year window, graduating from Princeton in June of 1914. He left Ol' Nassau weighted down with platitudes: best athlete, best hockey and football player, the man who has done most for Princeton." Shortly after graduation, construction was finally completed on Princeton's newly minted Palmer Stadium, a 42,000 seat state-of-the-art venue that would host Tigers' home football games for the next 82 years. Like Babe Ruth's connection to Yankee Stadium nine years later, Princeton's Palmer Stadium truly was the "House that Hobey Built."

But for all that Baker had done for Princeton, he exited New Jersey with a hollow core. On his farewell questionnaire, Hobey left the following items blank—political party and favorite field of study. Despite his gilded reputation as the pride of Princeton, he ached from a host of emotional ills: his absentee mother, his father's failing health and finances, and the staggering debt to brother Thornton for his college sacrifice. Over his previous 11 years, Hobey had transitioned from boy to man within the class-conscious enclaves of St. Paul's and Princeton, protected from each personal crisis by his sports-hero status. Now the 12-foot iron FitzRandolph Gate was slamming shut behind him on Nassau Street, and like Fitzgerald's character Tom Buchanan from *The Great Gatsby*, the biggest man on campus hadn't a clue how to deal with the rest of his life.

HOBEYQUEST:
BAKER'S STAND-IN

Because hockey statistics were not kept in Hobey's day, the man who holds the official record for most career goals (63) at Princeton is John Cook, captain of the 1963 Tigers. His photographed likeness accompanies Hobey's inside Princeton's gothic rink that bears the Baker name. John has never stopped playing hockey: for St. Nick's, the Princeton senior men's club, and impromptu games of shinny out on frozen Lake Carnegie.

John's late father Peter Cook, another Princeton man, is a celebrated American landscape artist. Peter was tapped to paint the ultimate oil portrait of Hobey, 40 years after his death. Cook positioned Hobey's likeness in skates on frozen Lake Carnegie, in full Princeton hockey regalia, blonde mane aglow. The finished product resembles a stunning Ralph Lauren model. It became the template for a popular trading card during the centennial celebration of college hockey in 1996. That painting, sadly, had been lost for 17 years. There are two other portraits of Hobey on the Princeton campus, one in Baker rink and the other hanging in the Ivy Club foyer, but neither captures the essence of Hobey like the Cook classic. Davies mentions the masterpiece in his 1966 biography, stating that it hung in the old Dillon Gymnasium, but it has long since been taken down, its whereabouts a mystery. No one from the Cook family has any idea where it resides.

I devoted much of a January weekend in 2015 to track down Cook's painting of Baker. With the Hobey trading card in my wallet and my undergrad son at my side—both useful chits in terms of Princeton legitimacy—I began the search in earnest. I hit the Yankee Doodle Tap Room, Baker Memorial Rink, the Princeton Art Museum, and Dillon Gym—no dice. John Cook suggested I reach out to Princeton's former hockey coach Guy Gadowsky, now at Penn State. He replied right away with an extremely polite email, but no workable intelligence. We were down to a final option, but it had excellent prospects. Princeton's modern Jadwin Gymnasium has several subterranean levels used primarily for other sports, but has one level just for stashing odds and ends. On the bottom floor, buried over 50 feet below Jadwin's basketball floor, was a locked storage cage, the final resting spot for Princeton sports artifacts. It was this, or nothing.

The gymnasium superintendent was kind enough to produce a key, and the three of us journeyed towards the center of the earth via elevator. Having been granted freedom to roam the cage, my son and I began clearing off dust and plowing through cobwebs; our search now colored by optimism. We found some classic Tiger sports mementos: a trophy honoring Dick Kazmaier, a broken frame containing future Senator Bill Bradley in basketball short shorts; a program featuring hoops coach Pete Carril exhorting his squad; but alas, no Hobey. My son was searching as well, but perhaps not as enthusiastically. The legend of Hobey does not hold the same place in the Princeton students' hearts and minds as it did a century ago. After exploring thoroughly but fruitlessly, we trudged back into the elevator, daunted, but not yet defeated. The lad went off to to study, I went off to play pond hockey on Lake Carnegie.

During my son's four-year tenure as a Princeton undergrad, I spent many weekends on the New Jersey campus. My longest running hockey chum lives in town on Lake Carnegie; we managed to enjoy quality ice time on one of Hobey's favorite shinny venues.

The Hobey Baker trading card that uses his likeness from Peter Cook's classic painting. (American College Hockey Association)

The world of senior hockey is an insular group; it is rare to play amongst total strangers. It was no surprise to find the good-natured John Cook doing what he enjoys most—playing hockey with friends and kin. To old-timers skating on Lake Carnegie, Hobey's name is not forgotten. An aging St. Paul's grad claimed to be the descendant of a Harvard goalie who once defeated Hobey. The name he shared did not match up with the historical record, but there was no need to correct him; it was reassuring just to listen to the lore of a man that time has nearly forgotten.

After an hour of recreation and perspiration, John Cook and I skated the half mile west to unlace. As we approached Princeton's Washington Road bridge, I mentioned to Cook that I had been searching for his father's oil painting of Hobey; neither he nor his brother had seen the work in years. I pulled out the trading card hoping to jog Cook's memory. As he studied it, he nodded, recognizing the setting of the painting, but it sparked no clues. Before returning the card to my wallet, I glanced at Cook, and then down to the card. It struck me that this live scene nearly replicated the image on the card—Princeton's top career goal scorer, helmetless while on skates, the bridge over frozen Lake Carnegie in the background. If this were the closest I would get to capturing the essence of Hobey Baker, I had little to complain about. Pond hockey in 2015 was little different than it was during Hobey's time, and neither was Princeton's Gothic architecture. I may have failed to find the original Cook portrait, but I had a more than reasonable facsimile standing before me on skates. I absorbed the glimpse of living history, a temporary moment of eternity, and then glided back toward the shore. [1]

CHAPTER SIX

The Sprint to the Hall of Fame

N o sooner did Princeton's FitzRandoph gate slam behind Hobey, than he was off on another madcap, high-speed adventure. Hobey and classmate Rolf Bauhan bolted to Europe and collected a pair of high performance motorcycles along the way. Bauhan, a slick operator on many levels, convinced the wire service *American Press Association* to fund the trip in exchange for regular reports from America's best-known athlete. [1] So the two men, fresh from graduation, sailed to England and beyond, tearing up the continent at dangerously high RPMs. There were two notable events when the boys got back to England after their last sprint through Sweden. One was their tour of downtown London, with Hobey weaving his way through Charing Cross traffic at top speed, dumbfounding the British Bobbies. The other was much more serious.

When Baker and Bauhan got off their bikes in central London, they noticed electricity in the air: newspaper headlines screamed *WAR!* as the young hawkers howled epithets at the German Kaiser. While the two Princeton grads had been busy touring the Swedish countryside, England had entered the Great War. Hobey, like so many of his fellow Anglo-prep products, was brimming with Noblesse Oblige, the sense of honor obligating the privileged class to fight for one's country during war

Although he shunned publicity, Baker posed for this rare photo. (Princeton University)

time, or in this case, the country of Hobey's ancestors. According to Davies, Bauman and Baker immediately tried to enlist in the English Army. [2]

Then fate intervened in the form of a Princeton professor who happened on the scene. He intercepted the headstrong boys and set about to change their minds. Hobey and Bauhan had long been conditioned to subservience to senior authority figures, and the professor convinced them that a sports star with an American newspaper following like Hobey would cause an uproar back at home if he enlisted, especially when President Wilson insisted on neutrality. So Hobey and Rolf took their motorcycles and reverted back to 'plan A,' hopping the train to Liverpool for the liner home. At the shipyards, they observed thousands of enlisted men boarding boats for France, patriotic young men who looked very much like themselves, getting warm sendoffs from beautiful women and loving families. Clearly the seeds of war were planted in Hobey that summer day in 1914. He had seen the eager determination in the eyes of each one of the men boarding those ships; there was no confusion of purpose for any of them. Baker, meanwhile, was boarding a luxury liner, heading back to New York and the depressing prospects of his fledgling career on Wall Street.

The nine-to-five working world was a massive downshift for Hobey in the fall of 1914, as he began his career with the insurance firm Johnson and Higgins, before transferring to J.P. Morgan and the banking industry. Hobey was the proverbial fish out of water. "Think of all the things I could do today, if I didn't have to go to work," is the line attributed to him on a typical weekday morning. [3]

If there was any spark of life in Hobey after college, it was the arrival of hockey season. Playing for the St. Nick's club after graduating from Princeton, teaming up with former mates as well as Ivy league rivals, in a venue where he had performed the last eight years, proved to be a reasonable facsimile of his days as a skating Tiger. And just as they did in college, Hobey and company won nearly every time out, regardless of the competition. Bolstered by its new superstar, St. Nick's went on a rampage, slaying powerful teams from both sides of the border. Lining up with longtime teammate Wendel Kuhn, Hobey and St. Nick's broke new ground, defeating every amateur club from Canada that they faced in 1914–15. This was simply unheard of. In the early 20th century, amateur hockey teams in Canada were nearly on a par with their professional counterparts. And regardless of who was or wasn't getting paid, in Canada's mind, hockey's balance of power always tilted north. They had the breeding grounds, the superstars, and the tradition—Americans were mere neophytes. But then came Hobey.

In Hobey's first season with St. Nick's, they played five of the best amateur teams in Canada, besting them all. Baker's impact was immense. He potted five goals and two assists in a 7-6 thriller against Toronto, and rang up three quick goals in a 6-1 victory over the Montreal Victorias, the defending champions of Canada's amateur circuit. In the season finale against Ontario champion St. Michaels, Baker set up each goal in a 5-1 win. This astounded the Canadian hockey establishment. "One man's brilliant speed, perfect skating and dribbling excellence alone offset the combined efforts of seven well-trained players from Toronto," was the lead sports story after Baker's virtuoso performance in Canada's most populated city. [4]

Modern pundits often try to put Hobey's hockey accomplishments into perspective by comparing him to NHL scoring ace Wayne Gretzky. Gretzky in his prime was the only man who scored at a rate even approaching Hobey's, yet aside from their respective point totals, the analogy falls flat. Gretzky lasted 20 years in the NHL by being clever enough to avoid the sport's hard knocks and meanest hombres. "The Great One" calculated where the puck would go, and would arrive ahead of the pack in time to pass or shoot before trouble arrived. He finished his career with more than twice as many assists as goals, clearly a pass-first, shoot-second player. Not Hobey. He was in constant contact with the puck, becoming the target of the sport's meanest hitmen. The best post-War player to compare to Baker was Bobby Orr.

Like Hobey, Orr loved to rush the puck the length of the rink, dodging most, but not all of the opposing henchmen. For all the glorious highlights of Orr, there were also devastating injuries. He failed to last a decade in pro-hockey before his once glorious body failed him. In his final bid for championship glory, Orr was hounded relentlessly by Philadelphia's NHL club, aptly nicknamed the "Bullies." They spent the 1974 Stanley Cup Finals intentionally flipping the puck into Orr's corner and then hunting him down. Their repeated attacks finally wore out Orr, and he was no longer able to generate the electric rushes that defined him. Orr's physical greatness ebbed before our eyes, and his Bruins lost a championship that most predicted was rightfully theirs. Due to his damaged body, Orr never played another full season after his 27th birthday. For all of hockey's breathtaking speed and shining artistry, it has an equally prominent nasty side. Brilliant puck-carriers like Orr and Baker were the frequent recipients of the sport's darkest arts.

All the success Hobey enjoyed against Canada's finest came with a symbolic price—a big, fat bullseye emblazoned on his back. Canadian players were representing the nation that invented hockey, and losing to Ivy League Americans was a public shaming. With wounded pride, they chased after Hobey and exacted revenge on the man who embarrassed them in their own rinks. The St. Nick's win over the Victorias in Montreal was a Pyrrhic victory for Hobey. Davies fleshed out one account of the brutality inflicted on Baker after he completed his three-goal hat trick. "He was tripped, checked into the boards, slugged, slashed, and finally when flat on the ice, kicked in the knee." [5] With St. Nick's safely in the lead, Hobey was taken out of the game for the first time in his life.

Baker was not immune from the game's brutality while playing in New York, either. The Irish-American Athletic Club team was filled with Canadian semi-pro's, proud men who couldn't stand the idea of being beaten by this golden boy. "We were Canadians being paid to play, and didn't intend to be shown up by an overrated, stuck up society kid," said one of the members. "We decided to give Baker the business, and believe me, we knew how. He was slugged, roughed up, kneed, elbowed and given every dirty trick in the book. Once our star, a big Indian center named Cree, banged Hobey's head against the cage and knocked him out for a few seconds." [6]

Incredibly, Hobey visited the perps' dressing room after the game. He had recovered and helped finish off the IAA with yet another brilliant performance. Hobey sought out each member of the Irish Association players, saying "how much he enjoyed the game." He made a point of approaching Cree, who offered a rare apology for bashing Baker's head. Hobey told him to "forget it, it was part of the game." [7]

Hobey's habit of seeking out his adversaries for handshakes in the locker room prompted the Hobey Baker Committee in 2014 to credit him with the genesis of hockey's most honorable tradition—the post-game handshake. It was sportsmanship at a macabre extreme.

Davies quoted another teammate who gave a chilling description of Hobey's nightly muggings. "The Canadians slashed, slugged with the butt end of the stick, knee-checked, tripped, and committed all the other personal fouls. During intermission, he (Hobey) said something to this effect, 'Those fellows don't want to play hockey, all they are trying to do is rough me up. This is no fun.'" [8]

A *Sports Illustrated* reporter from the 1950's commented

that the nightly beatings Hobey withstood were "masochistic orgies." [9] Not only did they take a toll on Baker's body, but on his psyche as well, regardless of Hobey's over-the-top sportsmanship. In his last team photograph with St. Nick's, Hobey is the lone man looking off camera, with a distant, unfocused gaze. Upon closer examination, it appears that Hobey's face is colored and swollen, and based on the accounts of the physical abuse heaped upon him, it makes perfect sense. Hobey's post Ivy League hockey life was a far cry from the gentlemanly encounters with Harvard and Yale; it had become a nightly war on ice.

During the 1915 off-season, Hobey enjoyed leisure activities, relaxing with his new roommate, Percy Pyne. The wealthy bachelor, ten years Hobey's elder, had been cultivating a relationship with Hobey since their brief encounters at St. Paul's and Princeton private club gatherings. Once Baker returned from his European motorcycle jaunt, he decided to accept the Princeton grad's offer to put him up at his Madison Avenue mansion. Percy's hospitality knew no bounds, and Hobey eagerly engaged in the carousel of summer sports that Percy offered: golf, tennis and something that truly resonated with Hobey's love of speed—auto racing. Percy organized races out on Sheepshead Bay on the southern tip of Brooklyn. It was here that Hobey met famous mechanic-turned-driver Eddie Rickenbacker, a gritty Ohio native who lived out Hobey's fast-car fantasy.

Percy also kept Hobey living the high life, providing him with a valet and other material comforts he would never have been able to afford. Away from the nightlife, however, Hobey's day job on Wall Street was a downer, stuck inside the vaults of J.P. Morgan, the "bowels of the earth," according to St. Nick's teammate Wendel Kuhn. "His job was to clip coupons for wealthy Morgan customers and I'm sure that didn't thrill him." [10]

As Percy Pyne's escort, Hobey had access to a second mansion on Long Island, and more country club golf and tennis then he could ever play. Hobey found himself assuming the role of Nick Carraway, the first-person narrator of Fitzgerald's novel *The Great Gatsby*. He was living and playing amidst the unimaginably wealthy leisure class of Long Island's north shore, all the while hiding the fact that he was a pauper by comparison. Once again, Hobey needed a shield to mask his secrets. This time, in addition to his athletic prowess, companionship to Percy provided safety from any uncomfortable truths.

There is an amusing, yet telling story of Hobey visiting a wealthy friend on Long Island. A servant presented Hobey with some warm water upon awakening, which Hobey quickly gulped down. Jeeves informed Hobey that the water represented the temperature of his bath. Baker was later forced to retrieve his sneakers from the garbage bin; that same servant having discarded them because they were so worn. [11] Even with Percy as his tour guide, Hobey's merger with the Gatsby set was hardly a smooth ride.

In the rink, however, Hobey remained the undisputed king. Saint Nicholas Arena managers Fellowes and the McMahon brothers kept putting the name "Hobey Baker" on their marquee, and paying customers continued to line up. Newspapers repeatedly declared Hobey to be a "One Man Show," making him the object of every opponents' defensive game plan—*Get Baker*. Despite skating as a human target, Hobey continued to perform superhuman feats each game, sending all the paying fans home convinced they had seen the best in his prime. The most remarkable aspect to Hobey's brilliance on ice was that he upended hockey's international order. Thanks to Hobey, the United States finally gained a foothold in the sport so dominated by its neighbors to the north.

"Starting in the early 1900's the feeling has always been that it's Canada's national game, and no other country can match them in ability," said hockey's most published author—and proud New Yorker—Stan Fischler. "So they nurtured this thing until Hobey Baker came along. I think the fact that they saw a guy like Baker, a superstar in the realm with their best—Cyclone Taylor, Lester Patrick, these guys—showed them that we're as good or better than them in various ways." [12]

The most prestigious amateur title on either side of the border was the Art Ross Cup, and the holder of that crown entering the 1915–16 season was the Montreal Stars. Due to St. Nick's remarkable run through Canadian teams the previous season, they were invited to play in what amounted to amateur hockey's world championship, the Ross Cup. It was a best of three series in mid-December, opening at Montreal's famed Westmount Arena on St. Catherine Street, the forerunner to the Montreal Forum. It was a cathedral of hockey that often crammed upwards of 10,000 French and English-speaking fans into its deep standing-room aisles.

Hobey was no stranger to Montreal, having played in hockey's homestead for both Princeton and St. Nick's in previous years. But the Ross Cup was truly the zenith of the sport, and the buzz surrounding the event was similar to that of a Stanley Cup Finals game. French Canada was not ready to accept Hobey's band of Ivy League gentlemen as true contenders for the crown.

For historians of hockey, this game had a vital rule change, one that provided Hobey with significantly more skating room. On the cover of the December 11, 1915 sports page in Montreal's primary French-language newspaper, *La Presse*, was a story hyping that day's game. The final paragraph contained a lineup for the game's two teams, and conspicuously absent was the "Rover" position. Hockey in Canada had just begun its transition to six players per side instead of the customary seven. In addition, the game would be extended to three 20-minute periods instead of two, creating a second intermission. Hobey was listed as a "centre" up in Montreal for the first time. [13] Not only were the dimensions of Montreal Arena larger than the St.

Nick's Ice House, but there would be two fewer players clogging the ice. As Hobey skated out for warm-ups, he noticed the exceptional glide of a perfectly flooded ice surface. A subtle smile split his handsome face.

With the eyes of two hockey nations focused directly upon him, Hobey proceeded to suck the drama out of Westmount Arena, turning the much-anticipated showdown into the equivalent of a master's music recital. The maestro produced five points, scoring two goals and setting up three others in St. Nick's 6-2 rout of the defending Ross Cup champions, a game that was not as close as the score. Hobey navigated the wide-open terrain like a sailor, tacking and jibing his way down the frozen sea. A few of the Montreal fans had seen him play McGill University and the Victorias in past years, but Hobey had never performed before so many, on such a big stage. Everyone in attendance instantly became Hobey devotees, delighting in his rink-length mad dashes. Baker's tour de force had stamped his signature dead center on the world's grandest hockey venue. It forced Canada's premier hockey writers to take inventory, and to acknowledge their American conqueror. This was the next morning's lead story in the Montreal Press.

> *Uncle Sam has had the cheek to develop a first-class hockey player. We had heard him advertised as a great hockey player and we had always smiled a cynical grin at the thought. He wasn't born in Montreal, Ottawa, Winnipeg, Toronto or the other famous breeding grounds. We refused to see how an American could win over such a handicap and arrive. A few minutes of Baker on the ice convinced the most skeptical. He could catch a place, and a star's place, on any of our professional teams. The blonde-haired boy was a favorite with the crowd. We didn't want the Saint Nick's to win, but Baker cooked our goose so artistically that we enjoyed it. [14]*

Future Hall of Fame coach and general manager Lester Patrick observed Baker's brilliant night of puck-rushing, scoring, passing, and defending over every patch of ice, and became starry-eyed. He stated that Baker was the only amateur he'd ever seen who could be a star in his first pro game. [15] Hobey was reportedly offered a pro contract for $3,500, an annual salary greater than most of the top professionals of the day, but he declined. Anyone who knew Hobey could have guessed as much, the idea of turning professional was anathema to Baker; pure amateurism was his vital code. He might have generated major dollars—for both himself and promotors—as an elite professional hockey player, but Hobey would never consider sullying his honor by accepting pay to play.

Despite the blowout, the Ross Cup series was not over. A controversial 2-2 tie the following week at Saint Nicholas Arena had New York fans grumbling for years to come. In their minds Hobey had scored the winning goal, but it bounced out too quickly for the goal judge to register it. The final game was another exhibition of hockey's ugly side, as Hobey was brutalized for 40 minutes, culminating with a vicious slash across his face in a 2-1 loss. "He was lucky to get out alive," said a teammate. [16]

Sixty years later, Bobby Orr shared Hobey's pain. Orr was badgered by the Philadelphia Flyers in the 1974 Stanley Cup Finals, a series in which his Bruins had also won the opening game convincingly. Like St. Nick's, the Orr-led Bruins were eventually worn down by their lesser skilled opponents. Woe be to the high-profile puck-carrier in an extended hockey series. There are images of the blonde, helmetless Orr, hunched over in agony as the Flyers celebrated on the other end of the ice. This is the closest approximation to what Hobey felt in his gut-wrenching loss to the Stars in 1915. Both men, Orr and Baker, were superstars in their mid-20's, both denied a championship due to hockey's brutish elements, the unseemly side of the hockey equation.

Regardless of the outcome of the series, Hobey had left an unforgettable impression within Canada's hockey establishment. If it's possible for a player to gain entry into the Hall of Fame based on a single game, then he had done it. The circumstances at the Ross Cup opener in Montreal—the large ice surface, the reduction of players, the stakes and the setting—combined to produce the ideal conditions for Hobey's wonder show. Like everyone else who had witnessed Baker's magic, Hockey Canada had fallen in love with the beautiful blonde man streaking across the ice with the puck glued to his stick.

Back in New York, Hobey's fame extended to everyone who read the paper: the gentiles, the working class, men, women and non-fans alike. Thanks to the newspaper-mad city of New York, the genre of celebrity had begun to explode. The publicity rankled Hobey, not because it wasn't true, but because it offended his gentlemanly code. He detested the idea of being considered a showboat. One night he arrived at St. Nicholas Arena and found his name plastered on the marquee once again. "Baker Plays Tonight," had become a veritable bat signal to his new legion of fans in Gotham, and Hobey had finally hit the breaking point. He marched into the managers' office in the back of the ice house.

"I'm a member of the team, and you're stressing individual," said the emotional Hobey. "It's an awful example to set." Wielding the hammer, Hobey slammed down an ultimatum. "I won't play as long as the sign stays up." And the sign came down. [17] Hobey's teammate Charles Dickey did not specify which manager Hobey played hardball with that afternoon. The very real possibility that the poster-child for prep glamor stared down Vince McMahon's father, with the latter being forced to blink, is simply too rich to ignore.

But Hobey's argument that he was merely a cog in the team's wheel simply didn't hold (frozen) water—he was The Show, a show no sports fan had ever witnessed in the early 20th century. Over his entire life, both on the playing fields and during the war, Hobey protested his fame, what he called his "cheap newspaper name." But his protests were pointless—he was a matinee idol with that unmistakable blonde mane, the player who constantly possessed the puck during his breathtaking "sorties" down the ice. He drove fans, arena managers and excitable newspapermen into fits of ecstasy. Gentlemanly protests by a single individual were not about to stem this tide.

In 1915-16, Saint Nicholas Arena enjoyed a second consecutive banner year at the gate; the managers of the Ice House were becoming rich off the backs of Baker and company. At the end of Hobey's last full season with St. Nick's, the Arena's management team—the McMahon brothers and Cornelius Fellowes—combined to purchase extravagant gifts for each St. Nick's player. According to teammate Rufus Trimble, it was hockey-loving Fellowes who presented every St. Nick's player with a "diamond gold medal, because of the crowds Hobey had drawn." [18] With precious jewels as evidence, the Hobey Baker era had been very, very good to the Saint Nicholas Arena hockey operation.

Rather than pricy baubles, however, the most important thing Fellowes could have shared with Hobey at the conclusion of the 1916 season, was his vision. Despite the Olympic movement being on hold since the Jim Thorpe Games of 1912, Fellowes had an historic brainstorm four years prior to the 1920 Games. The sport's most dynamic promoter would help make ice hockey a medal sport for the first time at the next Olympics. With Hobey stuck at a confusing crossroads in his life, the quest to play in the inaugural hockey Olympics, the apex of amateur sports, would have undoubtedly appealed to him. This could have given his life newfound purpose. But with the world at war, the Olympic five-ring circus was clearly on the back-burner. Hobey was much more curious about the Great War than Olympic hockey.

It's doubtful Fellowes even suspected that Baker's hockey career was coming to a close in the spring of 1916; Hobey himself hadn't made any decisions at that time about his future in the sport while pondering his dwindling options. Due to the gratuitous violence he had been subjected to on a regular basis, and his disdain for professional sports, Hobey could never have viewed hockey as a logical career choice. Without his knowing it, when the 24-year-old Hobey exited Saint Nicholas Arena at the conclusion of the 1915-16 season, it would be for the last time. He left behind a prodigious body of work throughout his decade on Broadway, dazzling hockey fans at St. Nicholas Arena originally as a 14-year old St. Paul's prep, then taking a star's turn with both Princeton and St. Nick's. For thousands of fans, three promoters, and the plethora of New York newspapers that fueled the fire, it had been a hell of a run. As "Hockey Maven" Stan Fischler points out, Hobey Baker was "the Babe Ruth of hockey." [19]

The Hockey Hall of Fame (HHOF) in Toronto did not admit its first class until 27 years after Hobey's last game, but none of the committee members could forget Hobey's breathtaking performance up in Canada. Baker was swept into the Hall as part of its inaugural class, the lone American among the dozen inductees. A phrase on his HHOF plaque captured for all time Hobey's premier skill: "Once the puck touched his stick, he never had to look down again."

In Boston, America's self-proclaimed hub of the sport, Hobey's sensational play resonated for half a century. Esteemed Boston essayist George Frazier, who was a mere child when Baker last wowed the masses at Boston Arena, managed to write a glowing tribute to the King of Hockey some 40 years after his death.

Always at college hockey games I am haunted by Hobart
Amory Hare Baker as he was in the sinew and swift-
ness of his youth, in the nocturnes of a half century ago
at the sanctified second when he would take the puck
from behind his own net and, as the crowd rose to its feet
screaming, 'Here he comes!' he would start up the ice like
some winged messenger out of mythology, as fleet and
godlike as any of them, his bright birthright a blazing blur,
and for a lovely, lovely while, God would be in his Heaven,
and the puck, more than likely, in the other team's net. A
legend is never easily come by; it is born and it grows and
it lingers because of a variety of reasons, but never is either
quality or color of itself enough. Usually it is a combination
of circumstances. In Baker's case, everything seems to have
conspired to insure immortality. [20]

Baker spent his first two years after college embossing his glorious legend on ice and gilding his ticket to the Hall of Fame. But now, with his love of hockey fading, Hobey had done nothing in those two seasons to address the nagging question that wouldn't go away: What would he do with the rest of his life?

For the first half of the 20th Century, St. Paul's school in Concord, New Hampshire was known as the cradle of American Hockey. It was there that Hobey Baker developed into America's first hockey superstar. The majority of the school's student body would play four months a year on the school's seven outdoor rinks. (St. Paul's School)

Hobey (right) and older brother Thornton from the 1908-09 season at St. Paul's. This was the last time they played formal hockey together until March of 1917. (St. Paul's School)

Hobey (left) and Thornton Baker entertaining the Roberts sisters of Philadelphia society. (St. Paul's School)

Hobey's Princeton Tigers won two intercollegiate championships during his three years of varsity play. Baker (center) was team captain his junior year, while classmate Wendel Kuhn (to Hobey's right) was captain their senior year in 1913-14. (Princeton University)

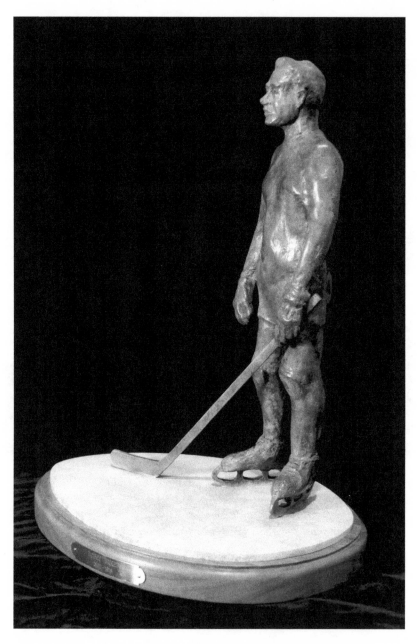

This sculpture of Hobey Baker was created by 1960 Yale hockey captain, Bruce Smith. It resides in the Hockey Hall of Fame in Toronto, where Baker was inducted posthumously in 1945. (Bruce Smith)

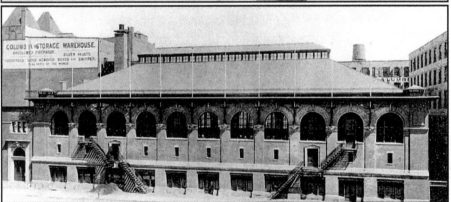

Top: During his two years with the St. Nick's Hockey club, Baker
(second from left) and company enjoyed such success against Canada's
top amateur teams that he was elected into the Hockey Hall of Fame.
(St. Paul's School)

Bottom: St. Nicholas Arena in New York City. Located one block
from Broadway, this was the predecessor to Madison Square Garden.
(St. Paul's School)

Baker Memorial Rink the home of Princeton Varsity Hockey since 1922. (Shelley Szwast)

Hobey's skates, notice the blades filed front and back, an innovation at the time. (Tim Rappleye)

*The Princeton home of Hobey's
father, Alfred Baker. Hobey and
classmate Rolf Bauhan spent their
senior year in its carriage house.
(Tim Rappleye)*

CHAPTER SEVEN

King of Hockey II

On February 9, 1951, Bill Cleary and his Belmont Hill prep team climbed onto a bus for the hour and a half trek north to Concord, New Hampshire. No schoolboy team had ever beaten the St. Paul's hockey juggernaut, a team that feasted on Ivy League freshmen; Belmont Hill was the only country day school on St. Paul's roster in 1950-51. In terms of reputation and history, SPS was the solid favorite.

It turned out to be a performance that mirrored Hobey's trip to Montreal 35 years prior. Like Hobey, Cleary was The Show that afternoon, setting up two goals and scoring the third in a 3-0 upset that shocked the New England hockey world—the first prep team in history to beat St. Paul's, up in Concord no less.

"It felt like we were playing at the Montreal Forum," said Cleary, referring to St. Paul's Mid-Winter Festival and their enthusiastic crowds. He vividly recalled the event 65 years after the fact. He'll never forget the playing surface. "That puck really flew on that black ice, we played outside, you know?" [1]

The St. Paul's newspaper account from the game lauded Cleary, much like the Montreal journalists praised Baker three decades prior.

"The period was highlighted by the brilliant William Cleary who was all over the ice."

The story went on to point out that "Belmont Hill began to use Cleary as a *rover*." [2] Only a St. Paul's sportswriter versed in hockey history would have used that term in 1951, a position that was long since obsolete. That was the name of the position Hobey made famous, a position legislated out of American hockey 30 years prior. Cleary had apparently woken the echoes up in Concord.

There was something mythical about that crossroads game—Baker's heir apparent knocking off Hobey's beloved St. Paul's School. Cleary's college career also mirrored Hobey's with his outrageous scoring totals. Back in the early 20th century, Princeton did not keep official hockey statistics. A quick exploration of the existing newspaper accounts, however, makes it obvious that Hobey compiled well above the magical four points per game mark, a statistical height achieved only by those on hockey Olympus. Just two men from the college ranks have ever averaged four points per game: Billy Cleary and Hobey Baker.

But unlike Baker, Cleary had no nagging doubts, no self-esteem issues. Screenwriter and former St. Nick's star Bruce Smith is convinced Hobey was driven by the absence of his mother's love, subconsciously pushed to be a star performer. Cleary, on the other hand, had a healthy family life and played like hell, purely out of his competitive passion.

In a poetic twist, Cleary was also front and center involving a crucial decision over his brother's hockey career. While Thornton Baker had to forego the sport in order to accommodate Hobey's dream of playing at Princeton, Bill Cleary threatened to boycott the 1960 Olympic Winter Games if his brother Bob was not chosen for Team USA. Cleary got his way, and two months later the Cleary brothers were celebrating their Olympic gold medal victory together in Squaw Valley, California. Hobey, on the other hand, experienced the bittersweet emotions of winning college championships and stunning Canada's best squads, all while his talented brother labored at home in the family business. Cleary and Baker may have been the two kings of American hockey, but they lived in stark contrast.

CHAPTER EIGHT

The Drums of War

Entering his third hockey season after graduating from Princeton, Hobey was banged up and burnt out. The joy of playing hockey for St. Nick's was fast dissipating due to the on-ice beatings he was taking in both Canada and the United States. He was also tiring of his role as Percy Pyne's squire, and his brief tenure at J.P. Morgan was coming to a close. Hobey embraced neither the culture nor the sedentary lifestyle of Wall Street.

Sports Illustrated's Ron Fimrite suggested that Hobey had much in common with the fictional character Tom Buchanan, the former Yale football hero in Fitzgerald's timeless novel *The Great Gatsby*: "One of those men who reach such an acute limited excellence at twenty-one that everything afterwards savors of anticlimax." [1]

Scholar Anne Margaret Daniel begs to differ. "Tom, in many ways, you can read him as the anti-Hobey Baker," said Daniel. "Hobey Baker, who in real life was a star standout athlete, chose to go away and serve in the war, versus Tom Buchanan who notably did not, he basically buys his way out. He comes back to be kind of a nasty, prejudiced leach on society." [2] The altruistic Baker is anything but a leach, eager to serve his country at the earliest possible moment.

In the spring of 1916, Hobey took a weekend trip to Sea Bright, New Jersey to visit Princeton classmate James Beck, staying at the Beck family retreat on the north shore of New Jersey. The two young men stepped out onto the back porch and faced the breaking surf, happily reminiscing about their days at "Ol' Nassau." Hobey suddenly became quite serious. "I realize that my life is finished," said Baker in a somber tone. "No matter how long I live, I will never equal the excitement of playing on the football fields." [3] It was a declaration that Beck never forgot.

This ominous quote has been used in every Baker biography, first and foremost by John Davies. It was unearthed in a letter written by Beck to Hobey's nephew Henry in 1959, 43 years after the conversation took place. It was culled and filed in Princeton's manuscript library by Davies himself. Beck concludes that letter with this foreboding thought: "I think he sincerely believed that, and his tragic death was not far off." [4]

Hobey's death was two and a half years off, to be precise, and Baker was poised to commence another pursuit at that very moment, one that excited him at least as much as the football fields of Princeton or the sheet of ice at Saint Nicholas Arena. Beck even mentioned it in that very letter, stating that he recalled Hobey was about to take flying lessons.

During the fall of Baker's senior year at Princeton, a Yale contemporary—William Thaw of Pittsburgh—generated huge headlines and a major buzz within the Ivy league community. In a daring stunt, he and his co-pilot flew Thaw's hydroplane up the East River, ducking under all four of New York's major bridges on Manhattan's east side. When World War I broke out, Thaw was already in France with his Curtis "flying boat." He donated that plane and his services to France's war effort, and by 1916 he was flying a French pursuit plane over enemy lines as one of America's first aerial knights. [5]

Baker commenced his flying lessons just as news broke that Thaw and a group of other heroic American flyers had skirted

President Wilson's rules of neutrality to enter the Great War. This band of Ivy League cowboys joined the French Aviation Service in an outfit known then as Escadrille Americaine, the forerunner to the Lafayette Escadrille. When news of their life-or-death aerial duels busted out across the country, it proved irresistible to Hobey and his ilk.

The vast majority of America's first fighter pilots were men of wealth and privilege, not unlike the medieval knights on horseback, Christians from the noble class. These 20th century flying knights were motivated by their powerful sense of "Noblesse Oblige," a creed that drove them into the Great War before the rest of the U.S. citizenry. Human flight was still in its infancy—the Wright Brothers had only succeeded getting airborne at Kitty Hawk a decade prior—making these World War I pilots true pioneers of the sky.

Six wealthy Yale men of Hobey's age and breeding spent family money—Rockefeller and Railroad Baron money—to purchase planes and flight training. They then formed an historic Navy Flying squad called, appropriately, the *Millionaire's Unit*, the basis of an enthralling book by the same name. Hobey also learned that his former Saint Paul's classmate Victor Chapman was one of the seven original Escadrille pilots when they officially formed on April 20, 1916. When news of their first destruction of a "Hun" aircraft hit the papers a month later, Hobey was already taking flying lessons with the Army Signal Corps out on Long Island in Mineola, and locally on Governor's Island in New York Harbor, half a mile south from his tedious job at J.P. Morgan.

Shortly into his latest pastime Baker learned the deadly stakes of this new game: on June 24, 1916, Hobey's SPS classmate Chapman was the first American pilot to die in World War I. Hobey recalled singing in the choir with Chapman his first two years at St. Paul's. His immediate response was to intensify his training; flying was no longer a hobby to Baker.

By the late summer of 1916, Hobey's routine now included bolting work early each afternoon to reach his 4 p.m. flight sessions. He actually allowed a reporter to quote him for a story. "I have taken up flying with a number of other college men to undergo military preparation," said Baker to a New York reporter, echoing America's World War I sideline slogan—*Be Prepared*. At the conclusion of the interview, Baker stated the obvious. "Aviation appealed to me more than any other branch." [6] Of course it did. Flying to Hobey was the logical progression for his other-worldly reflexes and evasive skills. First he conquered the turf of the gridiron, then the ice at the rink, now the wild blue yonder. Hobey's biplane would soon become an extension of his body, ready to engage the enemy in the greatest game of them all.

Hobey was consumed by his new passion, and whatever depression he shared back on that spring day on the Jersey shore had long since dissolved. He pursued his new endeavor with his signature enthusiasm, confidence, and conviction. In the fall of 1916 he quit his Wall Street job, escaped Percy's gilded Madison Avenue cage, and moved to Philadelphia, joining forces with his brother Thornton at the family upholstery business. By November, he received his preliminary certificate as a Government Aviator.

On early Saturday morning, November 18, 1916, Hobey was back in New York on Governor's Island, clad in his leather flying jacket and goggles. He discovered that he had made the morning papers once again. That Saturday's *New York Times* reported that Hobey had been ruled ineligible to play in the Eastern Amateur Hockey League for St. Nick's, because he now lived more than 50 miles from their home rink in Manhattan. [7] This development did not concern Hobey in the slightest. For months now his mind was on the Great War, and this day represented a huge step towards his latest goal. He and fellow aviator Philip Carroll were in their respective cockpits, scanning the skies to the east.

Observers up in wooden towers peered through powerful binoculars, and then shouted down urgently to the two pilots. Ten biplanes had just appeared on the horizon, and the two engines on the ground roared to life.

Minutes later Carroll and Baker joined the others in battle formation. The convoy of planes had just arrived from Mineola, 20 miles to the east. Together they were making history: it was the largest formation of planes for a military flight over American soil. They flew together another 50 miles down to Princeton, and then buzzed the Tigers' new Palmer Stadium, the house packed prior to kickoff for the Yale-Princeton football game. Hobey and company proceeded to bend the minds of more than 40,000 fans by performing never-before-seen aerial exhibitions. The *Times* reported that the group performed "evolutions in the air. They dipped, spiraled, and looped-the-loop. Each maneuver brought the crowd to its feet and brought prolonged cheers." [8] This operation clearly had Hobey's paw prints all over it, a chance for Tiger fans to cry out one final time, "Here he comes!" when Hobey's blond head leaned out from his cockpit, clearly identifiable to the throngs in orange and black. [9]

Hobey was the first to land, and hustled up to a seat in the bleachers. He was credited by the *Times* as the first American to arrive at a football game via flight. He and his comrades were impossible to ignore in their flying suits. This spectacle, referred to as "The Football Special," had become a trademark of Hobey's—performing public acts that required the spotlight, regardless of how humble and modest he was in person. He seemed terrified of being considered "cocky," but equally afraid of being ignored. His death-defying feats inevitably demanded everyone's full attention.

Meanwhile, Hobey's hockey career was drifting toward what appeared to be an uninspired close in 1916-17. Not only because he had been ruled ineligible to play for St. Nick's in the Eastern League, but also due to his disillusionment over becoming a target for radical violence during his post-college career. Unable to play Eastern League games, he skated occasionally for the Quaker City Hockey Club in Philadelphia and the odd exhibition game with St. Nick's. According to all published biographies, Hobey Baker scored the final goal of his sensational career on Feb. 22, 1917, a 2-1 loss to Toronto's powerful Aura Lee Club. It was an anticlimactic finish to his hockey life, a mere footnote in a season colored by America's anticipation of war.

World events now commanded Hobey's attention. In January 1917, the infamous Zimmerman Telegram was intercepted by British intelligence, and the news of Germany plotting with Mexico to wage war on American soil erased the last of President Woodrow Wilson's patience. By the end of the month the president sought from Congress the right to arm U.S. merchant vessels, and on April 2, 1917 he called on Congress once again, this time to declare war on Germany.

After his address, Wilson was mirthless, despite receiving raucous cheers from both sides of the aisle. "Think of what it was they were applauding!" said the President in the White House afterward. "My message today was a message of death to our young men." [10] Wilson, the ultimate Princeton man as both an alum and its former president, was aware of his alma mater's hunger for war. Other than the Army and the Navy, no institution provided more troops for America's war effort than did Princeton. The Tigers would shut down all their sports programs that autumn because so many of their athletes would be serving overseas. Wilson knew that the lion's share of the death sentences he had just handed out would go to Princeton men brimming with noblesse oblige, men like Hobey Baker.

A day after Wilson's address, Hobey completed the purchase of a 2.5-acre farmhouse in Southampton, 17 miles northeast of Philadelphia in Bucks County, PA. His new home was next to an airfield, where Hobey could continue training as a pilot and avoid the lengthy commutes to and from New York. His new property was a half hour drive from Thornton's family home in Bala Cynwyd, where Hobey divided his time before shipping out.

In the spring of 1917, Baker was an officer in America's Reserve Aero Squadron. Although reluctant to speak publically about his athletic feats, the enthusiastic young flier was quoted at length about his latest passion. "There is something about flying that you cannot explain," said Baker. "There is a perfect fascination in being up in the air. I have never been afraid. It just came naturally to me, and from the very first, I have liked the sport." [11]

Hobey was now champing at the bit to get into this new sport, eager to fight the Huns in mortal combat a mile high over the Great War's front lines. America had no infrastructure in place for their pilots in France, and Hobey had yet to fire a gun from the air, but he declared himself ready. He had positioned himself with America's first sanctioned group of aviators heading off to Europe to defeat the Kaiser, and to help save democracy for the Allies. He now had the perfect, albeit temporary, solution to the nagging question about his life's purpose.

On July 22, 1917, Hobey and Percy Pyne stood quietly amidst the commotion on Pier 62 on the west side of Manhattan. Together they stared in awe at the gigantic ocean liner the *Orduna*, a 15,000-ton behemoth that was in the process of taking on nearly 1,000 soldiers. Hobey's large steamer trunk was at his side, while Percy's blue Dodge convertible idled in the background, top down in the warm sun. Hobey had spent a final night at Percy's Madison Avenue mansion the night before. They had breakfasted and then driven across Manhattan together to the Hudson River. Once they said their goodbyes, Percy would continue down to Washington to work as a financier for the Federal War Office, while Hobey would steam across the Atlantic. The two men shared a quiet embrace, and then Hobey hauled his gear up the long plank. He found a spot at the crowded rail, and watched his best friend motor down the pier before swinging into New York's southbound traffic. Hobey's mind was racing. It was the last time he would ever see Percy Pyne.

CHAPTER NINE

The Fraternal Encore

Most of Hobey's last year before shipping off was spent with his brother Thornton, working at the Baker upholstery business and living at Thornton's home with his wife Marie and their child Bobbie in Bala Cynwyd. This was the closest the two brothers had been since they were hockey teammates on St. Paul's varsity in 1908-09, eight years prior.

They had been inseparable sports-loving pals growing up: learning to skate together on Wissahickon Creek their first eight years together, blowing off a family wedding to scale an oily pine tree outside Trinity Church in Princeton, shocking the gentile French by scuffing up the lawns of Versailles playing football while on family vacation. They appeared permanently bonded by their mutual love of sports.

But their lives veered dramatically after learning of their father's financial misfortunes while seniors at prep school. While Hobey got his chance to rewrite the hockey record books of St. Paul's and Princeton, Thornton majestically stepped aside, applying his considerable business acumen to resurrect the Baker family upholstery company. His noble gesture became family bedrock. "My dad went on to fame and fortune in the business world," said Thornton's son Hobey II. "He supported a lot of the family for many years. He was very much a hero in my eyes, and the family." [1] In the time it took Hobey to become one of America's first sports celebrities, Thornton became extraordinarily wealthy, a reported millionaire by age 25.

Part of the "family support" Thornton's son referred to was most likely the Bucks County farmhouse Hobey purchased in April of 1917, four months prior to shipping off to World War I France. Hobey could never have saved up the necessary funds to finance the two-and-a-half acre lot with his $80 monthly salary from J.P. Morgan. At the time, he was living and working with a loving sibling who could afford that purchase out of his small cash drawer.

Thornton was a good hockey player at St. Paul's, but certainly not great. He played club hockey until his senior year, when he made it to the varsity as a substitute. Thornton was in uniform that day in 1908 when Hobey wowed the New York sports world with his breakthrough game versus the men of St. Nick's. That was Thornton's only taste of big-time hockey, playing with his brilliant younger brother who was a second-time captain of the 1908-09 squad. After his Form VI year at St. Paul's, Thornton essentially retired from organized sports. There are paintings of him on horseback in a red riding jacket during what appears to be a fox hunt, but in Thornton Baker's new life, his competitive juices flowed within the rough and tumble business arena.

According to the prevailing wisdom of the late 20th century, the hockey career of Thornton Baker concluded in March of 1909. This was eight seasons prior to Hobey moving in with big brother and his young family in late 1916. A letter surfaced, however, providing evidence that the two Baker brothers were playing hockey once again in Philadelphia, almost a decade after Thornton supposedly exited the sport. Thornton's wife Marie wrote a telling note, circa 1960, describing an episode of her husband and brother-in-law getting together for some serious shinny in Philadelphia. Deduction tells us it must have taken place during the winter of 1916-17, when Hobey was living with Marie and Thornton in Bala Cynwyd. Her letter is another classic tale of how the sport of hockey can so often transform civilized men into feisty boys.

> He [Hobey] was devoted to his brother Thornton. Only time he lost his temper playing hockey was when someone tripped Thornton while they were playing a pickup game at a rink next to an ice plant on 59th Street in Philadelphia. They had some pretty rough games. Someone tripped Thornton, and Hobey was on him like lightning, and in upending him, his stick came up and hit Hobey in the mouth, knocking his front tooth out. I remember him saying to me so plaintively— "I just hope the dentist gives me a new front tooth for Easter." [2]

Then in late 2010, published reports emerged about a game Hobey played in March of 1917, an alternative history to the published conclusion of Baker's hockey career. The story first appeared in the December 27 *Pittsburgh Tribune Review*, days before the 2011 NHL Winter Classic that was staged at Heinz Field in Pittsburgh. [3] Local hockey archivist James Kubus and his partner Jason Cato broke a story that had been dormant for over 90 years: Hobey Baker played a dramatic farewell game in Pittsburgh's old Winter Garden. America's premier hockey reporter and author Kevin Allen used major chunks of that story in his 2011 book *Star Spangled Hockey*, writing how Hobey Baker played a final game for a Philadelphia All-Star team against a senior men's club from Pittsburgh, a full month after what the major biographers indicated was Hobey's official finale, a 2-1 loss on February 22, 1917 in Toronto. [4] Allen credited the *Tribune* and James Kubus' website, *Pittsburghhockey. net,* with a fascinating account of what proved to be a game that re-wrote hockey history. Kubus' sourcing was impeccable: multiple Pittsburgh newspaper stories and promotions from 1917. [5]

The fine print within these documents revealed another massive scoop: not only did Hobey end his career in much more dramatic fashion than established history dictated, but each of the newspapers listed a "T. Baker" on the Philadelphia roster. One paper referred to T. Baker as Hobey's brother "Tommy," a common nickname for Thornton. [6] Ninety-three years after the fact, the history of America's greatest hockey player suddenly had a fantastic final chapter, one in which Hobey Baker got a second chance to play a marquee game with his beloved older brother Thornton, on the biggest ice stage in Pennsylvania—Pittsburgh's Winter Garden.

On Saturday morning, March 24, 1917, Marie Baker drove with Thornton and Hobey to the gigantic Broad Street train station in the heart of downtown Philadelphia. It was there that the Baker brothers hooked up with the rest of their teammates to catch the train to Pittsburgh. They were scheduled to play the *Young Men's Business Club*, Pittsburgh's answer to St. Nick's, a team filled with former Ivy league stars. The Pittsburgh squad knew all about the *King of Hockey*, and couldn't wait for a chance to best Hobey Baker. Pittsburgh was one of America's most underrated hockey towns at the time, and this club was undefeated in 1916–17. There could be no better way to affirm a team's greatness than to claim a big-name "scalp," and these Iron City hockeyists wanted their place in history by knocking off the Baker brothers to cap a perfect season.

Pittsburgh played its home games inside their gargantuan Winter Garden, the world's largest indoor hockey ice surface—a whopping 300' by 140', significantly larger than today's NHL 200' by 85' dimensions. The Garden's surface more closely approximated soccer dimensions than hockey, by far the largest Hobey had ever played on. Keep in mind that Baker was in nowhere near the kind of shape he had been in during his collegiate prime. Now 25, Baker was a frequent smoker, licorice was his favorite snack, and had noticed a small pot belly emerging from under his belt. He and Thornton may have sensed that they were sharing a train ride into an ambush, but they were nevertheless thrilled to be making this trip together, shoulder-to-shoulder, in a big-time game for the first time in over eight years. The day-long train ride gave both men plenty of time to consider how much both their lives had changed over that time.

As the two brothers approached the main entrance to Pittsburgh's Winter Garden, Hobey saw a poster that rekindled the heartburn first sparked by promoters in New York and Boston: "Hobey Baker, America's Greatest Hockey Star."[7] Thornton got a kick out it, however, and gave little bro' a friendly elbow. Hobey couldn't help but break into a loving smile, altered slightly by some uncomfortable new dental work.

Pittsburgh's promoters set ticket prices at 35, 50 and 75 cents, reserving 1,000 of the most expensive seats. The *Pittsburg Gazette* reported a standing room crowd of over 2,000 for the Saturday night tilt, with first puck dropping at 8:15 p.m. local time. [8] Unlike the Ross Cup in Canada, this was an all-American affair, so the two squads played by traditional U.S. rules: two 20-minute halves and seven players per side. Hobey would be back at his familiar rover position, while Thornton was at the top of the list of Philadelphia "spares."

The Winter Garden at Exposition Hall had cutting edge technology to create the best possible ice surface. The Garden was only 500 feet away from the Machine Hall refrigeration plant, pumping a brine solution through 125,000 feet of pipe under the ice, chilling the cement floor base down to temperatures well below zero. [9] It created pristine ice, ideally suited for hockey: incredibly hard and smooth, with very little chipping or snow accumulation. In short, it provided perfect skating conditions for Hobey, and for most of the game's first half he morphed back into his dynamic best.

According to the local papers, the headliner hit the ice with his motor revved at full throttle: "Shortly after the start of the contest, after several sensational dashes up the ice, Baker opened the scoring after he skated through the entire Pittsburgh team, eluding the forward, defense and finally pushing the puck past goaltender Jack Chislett. Baker controlled the puck at will and every time he touched the puck, cries of "Here he comes," filled the Garden." [10]

The Pittsburgh squad soon righted themselves, eager to get the crowd back on their side. Marsh Herron, a Yale man, eventually scored for Pittsburgh to tie the game at one, just before the end of the half. It got the fans up and out of their seats for the remainder of the period, and the home team exited to a standing ovation.

There is no record of what was said in the Philadelphia locker room, but one can be certain that the Baker boys sat next to each other, Hobey's face red from exertion, framed by perspiration; Thornton fresher due to sparse activity as a reserve. Both were clearly pleased to be in this farewell battle together. Hobey had spent his previous two hockey seasons frequently getting smashed about, especially by the Canadian teams, without his brother at his side. Having Thornton here in Pittsburgh, if only for moral support, provided comfort. The Baker men slaked their thirst, took deep breaths, and then headed out onto the world's biggest sheet of ice for what they presumed would be a final 20-minute period of hockey. It would be double that before they returned.

The hometown septet resumed its surge toward the Philadelphia end to open the period, and the Winter Garden's capacity crowd aided the onslaught with its thunderous applause. Early in the second half, Jack Barbour converted the final shot of a sustained Pittsburgh flurry, and the Garden erupted. Pittsburgh's second goal in just over three minutes of playing time wrested the lead from Philadelphia, and it appeared that visitors' bluff had been called. They were hunched over sucking air, while the home team was buoyed by the Garden's cacophony. Pittsburgh's push continued, probing for the kill shot: "The Pittsburgers outplayed the Philadelphians, the locals bounding no less than 12 shots off of Ford's stick in the visitors' cage for near scores." [11]

Hobey was nearly exhausted. His exquisite cardiovascular system, the engine that powered his Hall of Fame career, had been neglected and abused since college. His three-year regimen of tobacco, junk food and revels with Percy Pyne represented a debt now being presented in bold red print: "Past Due." Just last month Hobey had come up short in his final game for St. Nick's in Canada. His penchant for roving the entire ice, in this case the world's biggest hockey surface, left him unrecognizably gassed.

That kind of physical extreme would have done in most mortals, but not Hobey Baker. This was America's hockey deity in his farewell performance. With his brother at his side—in uniform—for the first time in nearly a decade, Hobey discovered a reserve tank, and willed himself into a new gear.

Pittsburgh newspapers credited Baker with excellence on both sides of the puck that night. With the game about to slip away from Philadelphia, Hobey swooped deep into his own end to corral a rebound, finally relieving the pressure on his beleaguered goalie Jack Ford. Once Hobey gained full possession with room to operate, he found the fuel to proceed all the way down the cavernous ice, calmly depositing the disc past the overmatched Pittsburgh 'tender, stanching Philadelphia's bleeding. This highlight was a major plot point in the unfolding drama, representing Hobey's newfound strength. The game, now tied at two, was evolving into a classic.

Despite a plethora of quality scoring chances in the closing minutes of regulation, no shooter could solve either goaltender, and the contest roared into overtime. There were two contrasting forces this night: Pittsburgh's team play, which generated long swaths of territorial advantage; and Hobey's individual counters, forays that captivated the hoarse crowd. An armada of Pittsburgh newspapermen attended the Garden to chronicle Baker's historic farewell. Per usual, Hobey was front and center.

"Even the large ice at the Winter Garden did not deter him, the extra space made him even more noticeable," reported the *Pittsburg Press. The Dispatch* said that Baker stood out "so prominently with his spurts up the ice and his defense tactics that he was the most conspicuous player on the ice."

The game was becoming a marathon, reminiscent of the Harvard epic from three years prior, the night that Hobey became a household name in Boston. Like the classic from Boston Arena, this match also needed a third overtime period, its outcome to be determined in the sport's most dramatic setting—sudden death.

Due to the fact that Philadelphia had but four "spares," and that their roster contained amateur businessmen, not fit college athletes in their prime, it is almost certain that Philadelphia substituted for Thornton during the overtime. Thus the two Baker brothers were playing alongside each other in the world's biggest hockey rink, sharing the exquisite drama of sudden death before a delirious packed house. It clearly heightened the experience for both men. This is what Bill Cleary felt 43 years later at the Olympic Winter Games in Squaw Valley, a superstar playing at the zenith of the sport with his trusted brother at his side, something Hobey had been deprived of for most of his career.

There is black and white film of Bill Cleary's last goal in USA's Olympic finale in 1960, as he weaved through the majority of the Czech team before tucking in the golden dagger. Those might be the best "frames" of reference for what occurred deep into the hockey night in Pittsburgh, March 24, 1917, on the globe's biggest sheet.

All the newspaper accounts credit Hobey with collecting the puck behind his own net, over 290' feet away from the Pittsburgh goal, just prior to the 10-minute mark of the third overtime. Hobey did what hockey's great puck rushers of all time have done—Bobby Orr, Mario Lemieux and Bill Cleary—he went coast-to-coast. But none of those Hall-of-Famers ever went the same distance Hobey did, as the clock approached midnight in Pittsburgh. In Hobey's last act as a hockey player, he scored via the longest puck-rush in hockey history, finishing off an overtime thriller for the ages, with his brother at his side. The *Dispatch* provides the eyewitness account: "After unsuccessful efforts on the parts of the locals to cage a goal in this extra session, Baker broke loose again, taking the puck up the ice from behind his own goal and pushing one past Chislett that the latter thought he had stopped." [12]

And so it was done: in his final performance, the individual overcame the seemingly superior team, forcing his name into the headlines once again. Unlike that evening in Boston, Hobey emerged from this marathon not only victorious, but alongside his brother. It was a glorious farewell to the sport's greatest solo artist.

As Hobey and Thornton settled in for their 300-mile train ride home to Philadelphia the next day, a copy of that morning's *Pittsburg Dispatch* was exchanged. The headline in the sports page echoed a familiar theme: "Ex-Princeton Star Baker puts up Sensational Game, but has Anything but Easy Time Winning." Hobey ignored the story after seeing the headline, but Thornton perused it carefully over the course of the lengthy trip. Within the body of the article was the hometown version of the previous night's events on ice. *"The locals clearly outplayed the visitors, but the individual work of Baker, coupled with some clever goaltending,"* made the difference. [13]

Despite dozing off occasionally over the course of the lengthy ride, the two brothers were still aglow as their train pulled into the Broad Street station just before Sunday dinner in Philadelphia. They peered out the window, smiled, and hurriedly gathered their bags.

As Thornton stepped off the train he saw his wife Marie on the platform with their toddler Bobbie, dressed in his Sunday best, in her arms. The two beaming brothers enveloped them with a lengthy hug, none of the foursome wanting to break free from the emotional bond. When they finally unclasped, the men sandwiched mother and child and walked through the concourse towards the car, broad smiles carrying the day. The foursome sashayed past a newsstand as they exited the terminal. An ominous headline creased all the Sunday papers: "War Department Activates National Guard Units."

Woodrow Wilson would be declaring war on Germany in less than two weeks. The final chapter of Hobey Baker's life would soon be underway.

CHAPTER TEN

Who was Percy Pyne?

Ten years his elder, lifetime bachelor Percy Rivington Pyne 2nd, Princeton Class of 1903, will be known historically as "the great admirer" of Hobey Baker. In addition to being a wealthy financier, Pyne was an incredibly active club man in New York City and beyond, a member in good standing of no fewer than 47 elite city and country clubs for exclusive WASP society. He hosted an annual Christmas champagne dinner for the St. Paul's Bogue society, which is where he first met the pride of SPS athletics, Hobey Baker.

At the time, Percy's father was Princeton University's wealthiest benefactor, Moses Taylor Pyne, whose Drumthwacket mansion was the symbolic playhouse for the Tiger's most powerful adults. The entire Pyne clan treated Princeton's most exclusive dining club, Ivy, as a second home, another trusted locale where Percy and Hobey first engaged. Since Princeton and St. Paul's were essentially Hobey's extended family, it seemed entirely appropriate to the young graduate to accept Percy's offer of hospitality as he felt his way around New York his first year out of college. From Percy's perspective, Hobey was another sparkling entry in his bulging trophy case. Not everyone thought it was such a swell arrangement.

"I think it's too bad Hobey went to live with Percy," said Wendel Kuhn, Hobey's Princeton roommate, and a man who had known about Percy since adolescence. "He (Percy) was inclined to have a succession of 'fair-haired' younger men, protégés, and Hobey became one." [1] Kuhn was concerned that Hobey would become beholden to the older man, Percy's enormous wealth being "inconsistent with his money status, likely to spoil him for the creature comforts Percy could give him. I can't imagine Hobe being happy in such a situation—dependent, obligated." [2]

"Percy thought Hobey was the cat's meow," said Parker Packard, Saint Paul's class of 1955. "Here's this great Princeton athlete. When Hobey got out of Princeton, he didn't have much of a home to go back to. So Hobey stayed at Percy's, went to his job on Wall Street. At night, he would go up to Saint Nick's and play hockey, and Percy assigned him his own personal valet so they he could change into his white tie and tails and go out and have dinner after the game." [3]

There was a degree of symbiosis between the older man and his page: Hobey enjoyed the security of living in Percy's mansion and having a valet on call, while Percy loved showing up at his Long Island country clubs with the good looking and famous young athlete at his side. Hobey's Princeton classmate Rolf Bauhan said that Hobey had stayed at Percy's occasionally during his college days as well. [4]

Pyne was a valued member of the Princeton community. As a freshman, he won the 1900 intercollegiate golf championship, the first man from the class of 1903 to earn a varsity letter. After graduating, Pyne became his class president for four years. When his father Moses died in 1921, Percy was named a Princeton trustee for life.

Born into enormous wealth, Percy was a man who fully exploited his lofty position in life. His 263 Madison Avenue residence was a midtown castle with hot and cold running servants. And while he was an avid sportsman who taught Hobey the finer points of golf and auto racing, Percy was a singular star in Manhattan's leisure party circle, throwing bashes that garnered yards of newsprint. New Jersey-based author and historian W. Barry Thomson said that only Woolworth heir James Donahue could compete with Pyne as a poster child for the idle rich. [5] Pyne's mansion in Roslyn Harbor, Long Island was comparable to any of the palaces in the Fitzgerald novel *The Great Gatsby*.

Percy helped found the impossibly snobby Brook Club; his most memorable contribution was having the kitchen staffed round the clock, standing by to serve six-course meals 24-7 to its wealthy members. In its formal obituary, the *New York Times* described Pyne's grandiosity on the eve of the roaring 20's. It detailed a party that once again evokes images of the fictional Jay Gatsby. Prior to a formal dance at the home of his friend Cornelius Vanderbilt, Pyne threw a dinner party at Sherry's, the swanky restaurant on 44th Street and 5th Avenue. "The Sherry Ballroom was transferred into a section of a Paris Boulevard," wrote the *Times*, "with a line of cafés and restaurants. During the dinner, a sort of continuous vaudeville was presented, portraying the street life of the city." [6] Hobey commuted up from Philadelphia to attend that February 5, 1917 gala as Percy's guest.

Regardless of the man's reputation as a bon vivant, Pyne became a trusted and loyal friend to Hobey, a role much more evolved than the sugar-daddy he is whispered to have been. A genuine and powerful relationship developed between the two men. Hobey's letters to Percy from France during World War I are both tender and heartfelt. When Hobey's mom resurfaced in 1917, Percy is the only man on record to have visited her, doing so on multiple occasions. Although he frequently tried, Hobey's words could not fully express his gratitude for Percy's kindness toward the former Mrs. Baker. Hobey was thousands of miles away from the mother he never fully knew, and Percy's visits to her, a third person helping restore a lost bond between mother and child, signified something none of Hobey's other friends even considered.

Pyne's high-rolling fantasy life took a precipitous downturn in the 1930's. His fortunes began to unravel after the Wall Street crash of 1929, and he struggled to pay the steep property taxes on his princely Long Island estate, known locally as the "Rivington House." In an effort to generate much needed revenue, he posed for a magazine advertisement for Listerine Toothpaste. Included in the full-page ad were glossy shots of the inside and outside of his infamous mansion, a prelude to the 1980's television hit *Lifestyles of the Rich and Famous*. Inviting the public within the Pyne castle signaled a rapid approach to rock bottom. "That was simply not done in conservative society," said Thomson. [7]

Whatever fees he collected from Listerine were not nearly enough to satisfy his obligations, and in 1932 Pyne was forced to forfeit his mansion to Nassau County for failure to pay his back taxes. [8] For reasons not entirely clear, the career bachelor was essentially excommunicated by his family shortly thereafter.

Several of Percy's wealthy cousins, proud descendants of Moses Taylor Pyne, live in mansions throughout Somerset County, New Jersey. In 2009, the dogged Thomson sought them all out to learn what he could about the final act of Percy Pyne's flamboyant life. No one responded. Thomson finally tracked down 86-year-old Isabelle Russell Potter, Percy's goddaughter, but she chose to say nothing about the man known as Percy Rivington Pyne 2nd. [9]

Pyne's health soon followed the steep descent of his fortune in the 1930's. He first moved to Florida to convalesce, and then to southern California. Deprived of friends, family, and possessions, Pyne lived out his final years in a drab dwelling in the Los Angeles suburb of Sepulveda. He had no one at his side save a solitary nurse, who represented Pyne's only comfort as he battled debilitating illness. In his final act on record, Percy married his nurse with only days to live, the career bachelor seeking to share whatever remained of a once great fortune with his only companion. He died shortly thereafter, succumbing to a heart attack in 1950 at the age of 68.

Percy's lifetime of single living, and the fact that he lived with Hobey for two years in a relationship his peers have struggled to reconcile, led to whispers of an illicit affair that trailed Hobey long after he died. "I've heard sinister implications put upon Hobe's relation with Percy," said Kuhn decades later in a letter to biographer Davies. "I don't swallow that for one moment, don't believe it, completely out of character. I resent this sort of gossip and loathe the contemptible people who indulge in it. I think it's vicious and malicious. The fact that Percy never married is scant proof of what is inferred here. This is character assassination and it infuriates me." [10]

History will never read Percy's words about how he felt towards Hobey. Due to the loss of Hobey's effects, only Hobey's letters to Percy exist, not those from the older admirer. We know Percy wrote constantly to his younger friend in France, and generated a steady flow of gifts to Hobey from across the Atlantic: cartons of cigarettes, a silver case in which to store them, and dozens of Brooks Brothers underwear. Even Percy's mother joined her son in sending Hobey presents while he was in France.

Hobey was not afraid to confide in Percy about his heterosexual love life from overseas, or tease his bachelor buddy about suggestive photos of Percy posing with other women that he mailed to Hobey. Regardless of how their relationship manifested itself, based on Hobey's words and Percy's acts, there is little doubt that the two men shared a love for one another. The U.S. Army, after all, chose to notify Percy Pyne first about Hobey's death in 1918, not brother Thornton or father Alfred Baker.

We do know that no one honored Hobey more after his death, or did as much to preserve his legacy, as did Percy Pyne.

CHAPTER ELEVEN

The Great War, Part I
"Hurry up and Wait"

In the weeks and months prior to departing for England, Hobey's life had been one of frenetic preparation, including time in the air to learn his new craft. Once he shipped off, Hobey busied himself with shuffleboard and organizing a singing quartet with three other enlisted men. But his days on board were too long to find enough distractions to fend off his aching insecurities. After a single day on the massive ocean liner, he wrote his former companion.

> *Dear Percy,*
>   *It suddenly came over me as I saw you drive off what was really happening and I have not gotten over it yet. God knows I have not deserved all the affection you have given me. I feel, and have always felt, that I have stolen it from some other person for whom God meant it. I hope not. In any case, I am truly thankful.*
>   *Affectionately,*
>   *"Hobe"* [1]

This is the first of dozens of letters Hobey wrote to Percy during his time abroad, the man he wrote to more than any other from World War I, with the exception of his ailing father, to whom he wrote over one hundred letters.

For a man of action, Hobey was literally grounded upon arrival to Europe. First the *Orduna* was delayed nearly a week before getting into its berth in Liverpool, and once settled in Paris, Hobey and his fellow pilots were planted in desk jobs at the U.S. Army offices. His early months in the war were a case of "hurry up and wait." There was simply no structure in place for American fliers to get to the front lines.

"The whole process of getting things started from nothing to a smoothly running operation was a long and frustrating experience for all," said author Charles Woolley, whose father was a World War I fighter pilot. "There wasn't any air service, there wasn't (sic) any airplanes. They spent a lot of time sitting at the headquarters trying to figure out what to do next." [2]

Hobey and the other American pilots were in limbo, getting shuttled to various training fields in central France, safely away from the front until infrastructure caught up with the steady stream of new manpower. Hobey, finding himself with an overflow of free time, exchanged a series of sentimental letters with Percy during those early months. Starting in October, Hobey was transferred to the Cazaux shooting center, where he tore into fresh new letters from Percy. When he learned that his friend was considering coming to Paris, Hobey was beside himself.

> *October 4, 1917*
> *Got here this morning, to find two letters from you, and honestly, they were a delight to the soul. In one you said there was a chance of your coming over. That would be the greatest thing in the world. The good Lord knows how glad I would be to see you. For heaven's sake, arrange this if possible.* [3]

Percy remained in Washington, however, working as the

business manager for America's Council of National Defense. He took the time to visit Hobey's mom in Philadelphia, which clearly touched Hobey. "You certainly have been good to mother. Every letter I get from her is filled with a description of your goodness." [4] This is the first documentation of Hobey being in touch with his mom, newly remarried as Mary Pemberton Van Shutts. The fact that Percy was front and center in the most sensitive aspect of Hobey's personal life indicates the trust and affection Hobey had for his best friend. "Why you should be so good to me I'll never understand." [5]

Although they would take months to arrive, Percy let Hobey know to keep an eye out for shipments of cigarettes and Brooks Brothers underwear. Clearly homesick for Percy and his hospitality, Hobey's emotions often bordered on infatuation.

> *October 10*
> *Dear Percy, I had such a vivid dream about you last night, and it was so strong, it sort of stayed with me all day. I went somewhere to meet you and was terribly glad to see you.*
>
> *October 13*
> *Just received your letter enclosing the picture, and I was glad to get it. You look so clean and nice, so different from everything over here. It is so absolutely yourself, it gave me sort of a start to get it. If you were only here life would look so different to me. I am at present very depressed...I wish you had not sent me that picture in a way for it makes me want to see you so much.*
>
> *October 17*
> *I wish to heaven you would come over, it would be wonderful for us both.* [6]

When soldiers ship off to war, tradition dictates that they have a loved one at home, someone with whom to exchange sentimental letters, someone who holds a place in the heart of the man whose life is frequently at risk. It gives that soldier a reason to tolerate the extreme conditions of war, and motivates them to come home alive. Based on the tone and quantity of their letter exchange, as well as the thoughtfulness and abundance of Percy's touching gifts, Pyne represented that home-love character to Hobey, at least during the first six months of his World War I tenure.

America's first wave of fliers were under the command of the French Air Service, and while they waited for planes, these raw U.S. pilots were sent to the French hinterlands to train in both flying and airborne shooting. Hobey and company rotated through various training schools in southern France: Avord, Pau and then Cazaux. Lieutenant Baker was being trained far from the front lines, but was fast becoming an adroit pilot and an accomplished shooter. Hobey and former St. Paul's classmate Edwin Post, the eldest son of etiquette queen Emily Post, were the two outstanding Americans to complete the training in the fall of 1917. Post tested better in flying, while Hobey was the premier marksman of the group, learning the nuances of firing through a moving propeller.

"They shoot in every known way," said Hobey in an early letter to Pyne, describing the plethora of shooting activities at Cazaux. "Shotguns at clay pigeons, rifles at targets in the water, and at balloons. They shoot at silhouettes of machines on the water from flying boats, and finally at a target towed in the air by another machine." [7] In late October, those towed targets caused the first of several near-death experiences for Hobey in France.

While flying at 7,000 feet and firing at the target, one of Hobey's bullets severed the tow line, which jerked back, snapping off his propeller. The sleeve-like target, now freed from its tow plane, wrapped around his landing gear. In an instant, Hobey went from performing a routine operation in the air, to being snared in a deadly jam—free-falling with no propeller and severely compromised landing gear. He rapidly lost altitude and commenced what appeared to be a death spiral. "Those watching on the ground held their breath and gave him up for lost," said flight commander Charles Biddle. [8]

Relying on his athletic genius, Hobey survived the episode, pulling the nose up at the last second. The canvas target ripped free of his landing gear at the final moment, allowing Hobey to salvage the plane, and his life. His other-worldly reflexes and low-pulse calm had once again saved him. Biddle knew he had a star in the making. "Hobey was one of those who never give up and realize that in aviation the surest way to lose your life is to lose your head." [9]

Defying lethal danger was becoming routine for him, but not for the onlookers. "All the Frenchmen thought I was the luckiest man ever," said Hobey in that evening's letter to Percy. "I thought I was about to be killed, and it did not seem to worry me particularly." [10]

Every flier was surrounded by death in France; because of all the training accidents, the life expectancy for World War I pilots was reported to be two weeks. Two of Hobey's new friends from the instructional camps were killed—the training missions were as deadly as the trips behind the lines. Hobey wrote so many offhand remarks about what the allied forces called, "Going West," that one might think he had a death wish, but his sentiments were in lockstep with all his peers. Every pilot knew that the friend they were toasting and singing with one night was by no means guaranteed a spot at the bar the next.

Hobey's early letters to both Percy and his father frequently voiced foreboding thoughts about the War to End All Wars. He took a late autumn swim in the fog and the locals in the French countryside took him for an apparition. Percy heard a rumor through the slow-moving grapevine at home, that Hobey had perished in one of his high-risk training missions. Baker, growing ever more frustrated at being stationed so far from the front, appeared indifferent to his own demise. "Everyone new I see seems to think I'm a ghost. My being killed is a rumor that has gone everywhere…There couldn't be a nicer way to die… If I go 'West,' it would be a pleasant death, a quick and a sure one…." [11]

The reality was that Hobey simply longed for action. After getting breveted by the French Air Service first as *a pilote avia-teur,* and then as a full-fledged pursuit pilot in November, Lieutenant Baker hoped he might hook on with a French Escadrille and get a hot rush from flying over enemy lines. Instead, his flying and shooting prowess earned him an assignment to oversee 100 untested American mechanics, and afterwards, a slew of green pilots. This began a trend that frustrated Hobey for the length of the war. His dream of becoming a flying ace was constantly being stalled by promotions to new levels of authority and administrative responsibility.

Toward the end of 1917, Hobey and his pilots-in-training were assigned first to Gossport, England and then to Issoudun, France. Baker was growing incredibly restless; but all that time in the air, especially over the British countryside while stationed at Gossport, helped Hobey become a fantastic flier. He learned to turn, roll and dive instantly, his craft rapidly becoming an extension of his body. If Hobey ever did get any war action, he would be a force.

By the end of the year Lieutenant Baker was one with his plane. "You handle your machine instinctively," he wrote his father, "just as you do when rushing the ball in the open field." [12] But this was far deadlier than the Yale game. The deaths of three close friends in this war—Victor Chapman and two of Baker's recent training partners—made Hobey yearn to return the favor to the dreaded Huns. "If I ever get anywhere near that line," wrote Hobey to his father, "I shall certainly get a Boche [German], or he will get me. I promise you that."[13]

As he shuttled between France and England, forced to wait for his precious chance at getting to the front to apply all his deadly new skills, Hobey enjoyed plenty of random social activities. He carved out time for regular swims and even wedged in some competitive golf down on France's southern border. He described courting a lady at a Lord's manor, writing Percy how he was "making violent love to an English girl who seems to be enjoying it as much as I am."[14] In his own words, Hobey appeared to have settled any issues about his heterosexual appetite, ample evidence to support Wendel Kuhn's passionate defense.

But Hobey was not distracted by any lingering relationships, and he soon departed England. He then bounced around half a dozen training locations in the French countryside, treading water until he could find an outfit to latch onto and get to the front. The French had started mass producing Spad fighter planes, and Hobey knew his chances of getting into the action were improving.

In January 1918, Hobey connected with the gritty mechanic Eddie Rickenbacker, an old acquaintance who, like Hobey, was aching for his shot at the front and some real action. During that period of frustration, Rickenbacker and Baker performed stunt flying exhibitions together in Issoudun. Along with Hobey's Princeton pal Seth Low, the three men got in some deadly training at the start of the new year. Hobey's recklessness while practicing high-speed pursuits nearly claimed two lives—including his own.

The first instance was when Hobey rode up so close to Low's tail that he nearly drove his pal into the earth at over 100 miles per hour. Later, when Hobey was bareheaded without goggles, he was temporarily blinded by gunpowder, causing him to fly straight into an observation balloon. Hobey wrote the riveting play-by-play that night to his father. "It plastered itself on my flight wires and put the machine in a turn which continued until I tried to land. I struck one wheel, and of course the drift of the plane turned me over in a second. The machine must have been travelling between 60 and 70 miles per hours when I struck, and turned completely over on its back. Yet all I got was a large bump on my head, which knocked me silly." [15] Hobey's combination of blind luck and a matador's skill succeeded in keeping him alive once again. "I wish you could see how bold I am," was Hobey's account to Percy. [16]

Lieutenant Baker was not ignorant to the realities of war. He wisely took out a life insurance policy in case his luck should eventually run out. He paid $150 for the policy, with a conditional payout of $50 per month for 20 years, brother Thornton the beneficiary. Only one of three Baker biographers, Emil Salvini, claims that Thornton was given instructions to have the proceeds of the policy paid directly to the boys' mother Mary. [17] Based on her letters to creditors after the war, Salvini's assertion appears both credible and logical—Hobey's mom certainly needed the money more than her millionaire son Thornton.

At the end of January, Hobey's frustration at not getting into action was compounded when he was presented with a fresh copy of the *Paris Herald*. In it was a story of how he had taken down a Boche. Hobey was mortified, fearing how his fellow fliers would react to this patently false report about a pilot who had yet to reach the front. "Don't believe the news generated by my cheap newspaper name and notoriety," said Hobey in a letter to his father. [18] Seeing these fabricated headlines brought forth the same angst Hobey suffered when he read about his individual hockey exploits for St. Nick's and Princeton. On February 8, another story was brought to his attention. "That goddamned newspaper story," fumed Hobey. "I shall be killed by a taxi before I get to the front." [19]

Hobey's dad was living in Princeton during the war, and

reading about his son brought him much-needed joy. He was suffering from what was later diagnosed as *locomotor ataxia,* a degeneration of the spinal cord, causing him to lose motor function in his limbs. Despite Hobey writing his father about his distress over seeing his name in print, Alfred Baker could not control his pride, and shared Hobey's letters describing his exuberance from war-time flying with the editors of *Princeton Alumni Weekly.* They used all of it in a story they quickly turned around. [20] Hobey's commanding officer and Princeton alum, the exceptional pilot Charles Biddle, showed the story to Hobey, who was understandably crushed. He was forced to admonish his ailing father: "Please Father never again give anything I write to anyone for publication. I have enough notoriety now and people here do nothing but kid me and make me feel that I had a hand in every rumor of bringing down a Boche that has started about me. An article like that in the *Weekly* means to many a confirmation of their thoughts about me."

"You can't imagine how a thing like that affects me," continued Hobey, who was having his own doubts about how he would hold up when faced with death, miles above the cloud cover. "It all sort of forces me to do well, and I am not at all sure I can. I am terribly worried now that I will never be any good. I almost fainted at 5,300 meters the other day from the altitude, so please, never again." [21]

For a man haunted by insecurities and who also treasured his relationships with his male peers, seeing false reports and private sentiments in a public forum was humiliating. There were, however, some developments in Hobey's social life that brought him genuine happiness. During his occasional weekend leaves in Paris, he had reacquainted with Jeanne Marie "Mimi" Scott, a wealthy heiress and high society debutante from the mansions of Newport, Rhode Island. She was working for the Red Cross as a nurse in the hot zones of the western front. Hobey had met her briefly in New York through Percy, but starting in February 1918, Hobey began mentioning her repeatedly in his letters home. There is no doubt that he was smitten.

He made reference to Mimi in a letter to his father dated February 4, 1918. "I met a very attractive girl, seen quite a lot of her, and gotten a most decidedly and heavenly thrill. I met her before in New York, but have really gotten to know her here." [22] Four days later, he brought this new romance to Percy's attention, telling him how it was "…absolutely delightful to see a nice girl again. I spend as much time as she will have with me." [23]

When Mimi Scott wasn't being courted by Hobey in Paris, she was spending her time at the front, mending bodies of Allied troops. Even though she was from wealthy gentile stock, Mimi had been hardened by life's tough knocks. She was born in Paris to the French countess Jeanne de Gauville, who died when Mimi was still an infant. She was then shuffled off to her paternal grandmother's estate in Newport, where she lived a privileged existence without the comfort of close friends. Her bio echoed that of her future beau: a skilled tennis player, an experienced driver, a talented equestrian and a powerful swimmer. Back in the States she lived like American royalty, dividing her time between Newport, Manhattan, and Palm Beach depending on the season. Meanwhile, her distant father was making a fortune while living in the New York suburb of Tuxedo.

Miss Scott debuted to great fanfare in July of 1914, the same time Hobey was rampaging through Europe on his motorcycle. Shortly thereafter she learned that her father passed away from heart failure at the Tuxedo Club. Now orphaned, Mimi dedicated herself to French and Belgian charity work, and joined the Red Cross as fighting broke out in Europe. As America's involvement in the Great War became a forgone conclusion, Mimi took a crash course in nursing at a Harlem hospital. She was working 60 and 70-hour weeks in the hospital wards before sailing across the Atlantic in November of 1917, trailing Hobey by three months.

Unlike Baker, Mimi was fully trained and needed no costly equipment. She was part of the large contingent of Red Cross nurses piecing bodies together at the front. Mimi Scott was no dainty debutante. Described as both hard and cold, she led an intentional life in France, and one of her goals was to meet, and wed, a heroic figure from this war. Her sights were set on Lieutenant Baker.

Just as Hobey began writing home about the budding romance, his prospects of wartime glory improved dramatically. On February 8, the famed Lafayette Escadrille was incorporated into USA's 103rd Aero Squadron, and three days later Major William Thaw took its command. Thaw was a Yale man, whose brother Alexander had flown one of the 12 planes that accompanied Hobey down to the 1916 Princeton-Yale game in the infamous "Football Special." William Thaw was taking on pilots for the 103rd, and Hobey was a known quantity. He was so close he could taste it. But this was the Army, and unforeseen delays continued to plague Hobey. His occasional rendezvous with the graceful Mimi Scott were only temporary distractions from the inertia that rankled him as he paced the sidelines, desperate to get into the game.

Hobey's St. Paul's choir chum, Victor Chapman, the first member of the Lafayette Escadrille to die in action, had a telling epitaph: "He was addicted to danger." [24] The same could be said for Hobey. Every harrowing near-death escape amped him up even higher for the subsequent adrenaline rush. The next scene from Hobey's winter of discontent, his countdown to the true action at the front, illustrates a man with an unquenched thirst for thrill. Hobey provided this actuality hours after it occurred. It started with a simple errand—he and his mates were ordered to Paris to fly some Nieuport planes back to their base in Issoudun.

*Twenty-five miles from this place I ran out of gas and
my motor stopped. I had to land and found myself in the
middle of nowhere. I finally got a rig at a farmhouse and
drove into a town called Montmirail, where I telephoned
camp and told them on the map where I was. I got some
help and pushed my machine onto a road so that if they
sent out a car for me they couldn't miss my machine. That
night I spent in a farmhouse, and when no one showed up
from camp, rode a bicycle to a nearby town where I got
hold of the Commander of the French regiment stationed
there. Finally, in my best French, persuaded him to part
with 50 litres of gasoline. He put my bicycle on a truck, got
all his officers, and all of us returned to my machine. After
quite some difficulty, I got it going. Since I was on the road,
I thought I would try rising from it. I had trees on both
sides and telegraph wires, and I can tell you I had a bad
few seconds until I was clear of those trees and wires. Then
I turned and dove on those officers in the road and they
scattered like chickens. In about twelve minutes I was back
in camp.* [25]

Despite his claims that he did not like attention, Hobey
couldn't help himself, taking off with an absurd degree of difficulty, and then buzzing the French officers simply for the sport
of it. The *New York Times* published a story earlier that winter
about Hobey and his flying antics. One of Baker's sergeants
wrote in that he had performed a near vertical ascent, establishing a flight record while doing so. The last line of the story
was a telling one: "Brother airmen say they can recognize Baker
anywhere in the air by the individuality of his maneuvers." [26]

Therein lies the essence of Hobey Baker, a virtuoso individ-
ualist performing inside a team structure. Bill Cleary, another
solo maestro who played the ultimate team sport, knows all
about the delicate balance between team and individual. "He
knew he was an outstanding player, and yet he knew he was part

of a team," said the fellow *rover*. "That's a rare commodity, and he understood that." [27] What Hobey understood best, was that he lived to break away from the team, and feel the rush of wind in his blonde mane.

Finally, Hobey got his breakthrough. Not only did major Thaw find a spot for Hobey in the famed 103rd Aero Squadron (at the time still known as the Lafayette Escadrille), but he put Hobey under the command of his good friend and fellow Princeton man Charles Biddle. Baker joined his new outfit near Dunkirk in April of 1918, up on France's northern border with Belgium. Knowing that his good pal and training partner Eddie Rickenbacker had just experienced his first flight over enemy lines on April 6, Hobey was ecstatic when he jumped into Biddle's two-seater for his maiden voyage six days later. His initial trip, sitting wide-eyed at the hip of his commanding officer, contained a month's worth of action. Hobey absorbed every ounce of it alongside the steely veteran.

Minutes after crossing into German controlled territory, Hobey learned a whole new meaning of turbulence. He was nearly launched out of his seat by anti-aircraft explosions adjacent to the cockpit at 10,000 feet. Once they cleared the "Archies [anti-aircraft]," Biddle patiently taught Hobey the proper mindset while seeking out enemy aircraft at different altitudes, even with the sun in one's eyes. Biddle compared it to duck hunting, how what appears to be nothing is often something. Biddle then spotted a couple of Huns thousands of feet above them, where moments earlier Hobey had seen nothing. Baker then witnessed a natural born killer go about his lethal business. Biddle hunted down the enemy biplane with deadly intent, raking the German Albatross with a flurry of bullets, killing the pilot and then circling back to finish off the observer.

"Yeah, I was scared up there," said Hobey to his dad in his nightly letter, "but there couldn't be a nicer way to die." [28]

After what had seemed like an endless wait, Hobey had finally found true—albeit temporary—happiness on the front lines in the middle of a world war. "Well, this is at last the front," said Hobey to Percy. "I'm courting danger daily, living the storybook life of a daring aviator." [29] He enjoyed Ivy League camaraderie in the Allies' most glamorous outfit, his appetite for life and death thrills was fed daily, and when rewarded with well-earned leaves, he had the "right" woman to lick his wounds in the City of Light. Bolstered by the confidence from having attained a perch with the glamorous Lafayette Escadrille, Hobey revealed to his father that Mimi Scott would "certainly do for a wife." [30]

Lieutenant Baker was glowing when he returned to base with Biddle the evening of April 12, but whatever buzz Hobey felt from his first encounter with the enemy, it was but a soft hum compared to the full-throated roar that awaited him.

CHAPTER TWELVE

The Great War, Part 2
"The Varsity"

Hobey's life with the 103rd Aero Squadron in the spring of 1918 was exactly where he wanted to be, but it was hardly idyllic. Unlike the Hollywood imagery, the barracks of the Lafayette Escadrille were Spartan and his lifestyle nomadic, as Hobey frequently wrote about how he had to pack up and move on short notice. His plane was constantly in ill-repair and bad ammo continued to jam his gun. He ate poorly and rarely slept more than five hours, as first mission of the day was always pre-dawn. Also, Hobey rarely found the action that he craved; he spent much of his patrol time struggling for visibility through aggravating cloud cover. But there was no place on earth he would rather be, having finally made the *varsity*, with danger constantly lurking, whether visible or not. "This certainly is a big-league game, and I love it," wrote Hobey to his father. [1]

Shortly after sharing those sentiments, Hobey nearly lost his commanding officer. Flying in tandem, Hobey trailed Charley Biddle when they spotted an enemy biplane low to the ground, deep in German territory. Biddle attacked, and Hobey faithfully covered from the rear, despite his low fuel and a compromised engine. The primary combatants took turns attacking and defending. After the last exchange, they were less than 1,000 feet above the ground. Hobey continued to cover, but was on reserve fuel. Biddle went into a diving turn, gliding toward the Allied lines. The last thing Hobey saw was Biddle landing in no-man's-land, his plane turning over. [2] Desperately low on petrol, Hobey abandoned his friend, and scrambled back to base.

A day later, Hobey and two other fliers went searching for Biddle in the war-torn village of Ypres, and discovered him waving to them from an ambulance. It turned out that Biddle had just endured a hair-raising 24 hours in no-man's land, zig-zagging on foot from shell-hole to bunker, serenaded by exploding shells and machine gun fire before finally sprinting the last 50 yards on a bum leg toward the safety of a British out-post. The Belgian hospital found enough bullets nestled in his leg to ground him temporarily. [3] Hobey would now be patrolling behind enemy lines without his trusted mentor for the foresee-able future; a tenuous future at that, best taken a day at a time.

Rather than keep a journal *and* write to several parties back home, Hobey consolidated his writing almost exclusively in letters to his father, who became Hobey's information clearing-house. On May 21, Hobey checked in after his 6-8 a.m. tour: "I miss Charley Biddle sorely," penned Hobey. "There were some Boche over our heads, Albatross, but I never saw them." Hobey finished his note by describing the mission as "uninteresting." [4]

His subsequent flight that evening, on the other hand, was the most exciting two hours Hobey had ever experienced on earth, or more accurately, a mile above it. His hands were trembling when he put pen to paper.

It was the biggest thrill I ever had in my life! I am still all
excited over it just as I used to be after a big game. We
went way into Boche lines over their balloons. I don't think
I got a Boche but I came very close...I am a liar, a liar a

liar…Report just came in we got two of them, just as I was writing this. Two have been confirmed and I am wild with joy. No one knows which one of us got them because it was such a tremendous fight… after you shot and pulled away you hadn't time to watch the effect of your shots for you were twisting and dodging the Boche who was shooting on your tail. I am so excited I can hardly write. There were six of us in the patrol, and we ran into a cloud of Boche, about 30 in the bunch. They were at all heights between 5,000 and 3,000, we immediately attacked. I got on the tail of a big Albatross and let my gun run steadily, 160 shots at him. Suddenly I looked up and found a little Boche tri-plane on my tail. I dove and twisted, then found another Albatross below me and went for him. There were only six of us against 30 or so of them and we would have been swamped, but some English Dolphins and French Spads came along and gave us a hand. The Boche went into their lines.

I wish you could have seen that fight. It looked like some wild picture of battle contortions you see at home in maga-zines, some with wheels pointed up instead of down, some climbing steeply in big turns, some diving with another on his tail. It was so exciting, I forgot to be scared. [5]

Hobey was vibrating from lighting up his neural pleasure centers once he got back to base. He couldn't fall asleep for several hours after his triumphant night—multiple downed planes without "big brother" Biddle at his side.

The awarding of dogfight 'kills' was quite political in World War I; credit for that evening's destruction of German planes was given out, taken back and finally returned. It was months later that Hobey's scorecard was finally credited with a partial kill. This trial by fire eventually earned Hobey both his Croix de Guerre and a commendation from General Pershing for bravery under enemy fire. No one could possibly question their legitimacy after that epic dogfight over Ypres.

Hobey emerged from this rite of passage a changed man: he now knew first-hand the meaning of life and death in aerial pursuit on a massive scale. This was his first hit of heroin; he would spend the rest of his life doing what addicts call *chasing the dragon*, trying to replicate the high from that first mind-bending experience, an impossible task.

Hobey overslept the next day, missing another blazing battle in the sky, which he regretted. Five men in his patrol set out and engaged eight German counterparts; only three Allies returned. A day later Hobey had finally come down from the battle high, his manic pendulum swinging back toward darkness. He began taking inventory of his love-life, and how it might manifest itself during a post-war relationship. That night he was blunt with his father.

"I wish she did not have so much money, and I had more… what will I do if I live through this war? I am worth about a Franc a week to Thornton. We will figure on living through this war, but really, the chances are not good." [6]

As Hobey fell deeper in love with Mimi throughout the spring and summer of 1918, he shared his fear of financial inadequacy in a note to Percy. "Wouldn't it be queer if I ever lived through the war and tried to get her to marry me? What in 'ell I would marry her on I don't know." [7]

When he wasn't high from combat, Hobey's personality would fluctuate between fatalistic to full on depression. Seeing Mimi on special leaves to Paris would always lift his spirits, but she was intensely busy at the Compiegne hospital 50 miles north of Paris, her schedule rigid. Their visits together were intense, but infrequent.

June 1918 was another month of frustration for Lieutenant Baker. The various Spad aircraft he was assigned to fly were wonky, and frequently out of commission. When Hobey did manage to get airborne, it was often in a machine with compromised engine power due to faulty fuel delivery. Yet he continued to keep himself alive, despite his propensity to ignore risk and steep odds. On June 23, he wrote Percy: "I have a plane I am not very crazy about, but maybe in time I shall get used to it. Today the Boche (anti-aircraft) put a piece of shrapnel clean through the fuselage, missing my rudder wire by four inches. The weather has been very bad, so that we have little flying. I have certainly done nothing as yet to be very proud of, but I have never let an opportunity go by to try and get a Boche." [8]

Hobey coordinated a leave from the front and met Mimi in Paris, a long weekend (July 5-8) that put his relationship on new ground. After a year of being deprived of the comforts of home, the two lovers gloried in clean sheets, hot baths and Parisian restaurant meals together. Hobey gushed in his next letter to Percy. "The most wonderful thing that has happened to me in a long while." [9] Although they withheld announcements until the end of summer, it was that weekend in Paris when Hobey and Mimi made a pact: should they survive this awful war, they would spend the rest of their lives together. Mimi had just been evacuated from her Compiegne hospital due to German shelling, and Hobey faced death daily. The idea of extending their blissful romance, surrounded by silk and scented soap at the time of the proposal, was a heavenly fantasy amidst wartime despair. Had Hobey consulted his mentor, Charley Biddle, he might have reconsidered.

Biddle met Mimi at lunch that summer in Paris. "She was a good-looking girl in a flashy sort of way," wrote Biddle. "But my impression of her was that she was hard and had no sweetness. To me she had no charm at all, and I remember being very dubious of Hobey's prospects for happiness if he should marry her." [10]

Biddle never shared those sentiments with Hobey; they were busy trying to prosecute a war. Biddle felt a great affinity for his fellow Princeton Tiger, and was convinced that Hobey had all the makings not only of a first-class pilot, but as a leader of men. Days after Hobey's romantic rendezvous in Paris, Biddle promoted Hobey to flight commander of the 13th Aero Squadron's second pursuit group. It separated Hobey from the Lafayette Escadrille, but it provided what both Biddle and Hobey hoped would be Baker's best opportunity for military glory. Americans that forged reputations as war heroes generated huge prestige for the soldier's entire clan. For Hobey, that meant bringing much-needed joy to his ailing father back home in Princeton.

But as had been the case so often during Hobey's tenure in France, he was plagued by military SNAFUs: faulty equipment, manpower shortages and inadequate ground facilities. He found himself borrowing planes on the rare days he did get airborne, or relegating himself to 24-hour ground control out of senior duty. And as was becoming a frustratingly regular occurrence for Hobey, he was forced to wait out long weather delays.

There was one highlight in a letter to his dad, where he and two others believed to have combined to down a Boche on July 20, but it was later rescinded. Adding to his angst was more bogus newspaper reporting of his aerial exploits. The International News Service ran a picture of him underneath the headline "Gridiron Star Baker is Now an American Ace," [11] crediting him with five kills before he had officially downed a single Hun. The leaky source, though never outed as such, was most likely Hobey's dad once again. Reporters knew that Alfred Baker was on the receiving end of all of Hobey's letters, and that proud Papa couldn't contain his loose lips. Seeing the hyperbole in print always pained Hobey; he would inevitably get teased by his fellow pursuit pilots. And he was having a hell of a time simply getting airborne for the chance to ring up some legitimate scores. A thousand American cigarettes and a case of Brooks Brothers underwear arriving from Percy Pyne did little to cure the blues of this grounded pilot.

A recap of his letters home during his time with the 103rd read like a gambler who can't catch a break: July 19—Engine pressure forces him to abort all three of his patrols; July 22—"Motor heated up, had to come in;" August 3—Forced to borrow a plane, perfect day for flying, no Germans in sight, "Stale and discouraged;" August 4—"Did not go out;" August 5—"Supremely dull;" August 6—"Rainy and cloudy all day." [12] Borrowing the vernacular from this war, Hobey was having a stretch of "Rum Luck."

Although he failed to rack up prestigious kill totals with the likes of Raoul Lufbery and his buddy Eddie Rickenbacker, Hobey remained the apple of the eye of not only of his commanding officer Biddle, but Major William Thaw as well. Both Thaw and Biddle did everything in their considerable power to cushion Hobey's intense frustrations. On August 8, not only did Colonel Thaw grant Hobey a three-day leave to see Mimi, but he lent him his personal car *and* his sister's country home in Brise. In the middle of a maddening war, Hobey once again found romantic bliss.

"Had a most wonderful time," wrote Hobey to his father about his dalliance in the French countryside. "It was absolutely ideal." [13] From Mimi's perspective, it must have been a fantastic break from her daily life in the blood-soaked emergency rooms of Compiegne hospital. Sharing carnal pleasures with the man compared to a Greek god must have been intoxicating, even for the woman whom Biddle described as having "no sweetness." It is entirely plausible that under these circumstances, the product of the Newport mansions was sincere when she agreed to marry this man of limited means. How that choice held up in the harsh light of reality was another matter altogether.

When Hobey returned to base after his virtual honeymoon, Charley Biddle had administered his political capital yet again on behalf of his young friend. Lieutenant Baker learned that he was being transferred anew to the 141st Squadron. Only this time he would be its commanding officer, a significant promotion that would result in a captaincy, if he could make the grade. It did not jump-start Hobey's endorphins, however. Just as he was getting established on the front once again as a flier, he was now hopping a train back into the French interior to receive his official orders. These newly assigned duties, administrative obligations that required foresight and long-term calculations, were something more in line with his older brother's skill set. "This means a lot of work and responsibility," Hobey wrote his father, "a chance to use my head if such a thing exists. I am going to try and run it as Thornton would." [14] Hobey knew of what he spoke: Thornton, at the time of that letter, had turned the once dormant family upholstery business into a thriving profit center.

For the younger brother who yearned for a chance at glory, whose mindset rarely veered beyond one day and the next, this promotion to the adult world of long-term planning was grim news. He was now exiting the front, the dogfighting dispatch center that had taken Hobey months to get to. For the remainder of the war, the swashbuckling Hobey Baker would be more administrator than deadly pursuit pilot. But he was a loyal company man, and resigned to his fate, he boarded the southbound train.

As Hobey processed his latest uprooting, he diverted to Paris to collect some stray belongings before moving on to Tours and his latest destiny. He enjoyed trips to Paris and gathering with the American expats who were rapidly becoming his extended family. He was known on a first-name basis at several points of call: the Maurice hotel, the Crillon Hotel bar—the preferred watering hole for Allied aviators—and one extravagant apartment in downtown Paris. American songwriting phenom Cole Porter had become a social whirlwind in the City of Light during the final year of World War I, and his musical gifts enticed Hobey to several of his parties over the summer of 1918. Ordinarily, attending a party in Paris would hardly be noteworthy, except that these were no ordinary parties. These were Cole Porter bashes, hosted by the man who threw the most outrageous soirees in a city that knew no limits.

Porter and Baker were Ivy League contemporaries: Cole was a Yale football worshipper during Hobey's run at Princeton. While Baker was a prodigious point producer for the Tigers' football and hockey squads, Porter was even more productive churning out songs during his time in New Haven, including the immortal Eli football anthem "Bulldog" ("Bulldog! Bulldog! Bow, wow, wow," goes the refrain.) Porter's internet biography reveals the extent of the debauchery of the very parties Hobey attended that summer: "Porter maintained a luxury apartment in Paris, where he entertained lavishly. His parties were extravagant and scandalous, with much gay and bisexual activity, Italian nobility, cross-dressing, international musicians and a large surplus of recreational drugs." [15]

Hobey's August 15 note to his father, which had become his de facto journal, included this non-descript entry: "Took the morning train to Paris on the 13th, and had quite a party with Cole Porter at his apartment, where we sang, and he played. He is very good." [16] Biographer Salvini wrote about Hobey attending one of the parties hosted by Cole Porter, "who was holding court in Paris wearing a bogus custom-made uniform in order to impress his guests and convince them that he was actually in the service." [17]

The only men Porter worshipped more than Ivy League football jocks were the Knights of the Sky, the dashing aerial pursuit pilots that were comprised almost entirely of Ivy League sports heroes. Porter, a barely concealed closet homosexual at the time, falsely claimed to be a recruiter for the Department of

American Aviation. It's logical that he used his parties for active recruitment of one form or another.

Hobey and Porter both sang for their respective glee clubs in college, and Hobey's favorite pastime was to croon in harmony with others. There is little doubt that Hobey sidled up to Porter's piano that night, and that Porter flirted with Baker. Hobey was probably immune to male admiration; his physique and exploits on the playing fields had long made him the object of desire from both genders. On the night of August 13, 1918, Hobey was without his paramour in the city where they had fallen in love, entering Porter's party in low spirits. He was suddenly lavished with attention, sparkling wine and the joy of song. "We sang, and he played." Hobey's next recorded act was making the next day's 2:35 p.m. train for the ten-hour slog to Tours.

After arriving in Tours, Hobey spent the majority of the following morning waiting to see Colonel Hiram Bingham. When he finally got his audience with the scholarly Yale man, the news Hobey spent half a day waiting to hear could not have been worse. "They made a mistake in sending for me so soon," Hobey journaled to his father. "The squadron I am to command is at present still in England. That means about two months at least before I get back to the front. It is discouraging. Always the same, delay and mistake." [18]

Despite the latest setback, Hobey remained a diligent soldier. Fourteen years of towing the line in Episcopal prep schools and college had bred enough conformity into Hobey to keep him from doing anything rash; he was no loose cannon. While waiting for his troops, he scouted out temporary locations for his men of the 141st, and made inquiries for a permanent aerodrome at the overly crowded front. While trying to sort out the tangle of military red tape, Hobey went three weeks without seeing Mimi. Depression set in once again.

Hobey journaled his father that he attended another Cole Porter bash on August 20. [19]

Finally, on the evening of August 28, Hobey's entire squadron, 850 men and officers, piled onto northbound box cars for a train ride to yet another holding location, his first trip with his green troops. He had reached the nadir of his war career. "It is no fun," wrote Hobey. "The trains are unbelievably slow. Thornton could have made the trip in his old Ford in five hours. It took us close to 24, with no regular meals. I'm afraid we shall be here indefinitely. Fields at the front are not prepared for more squadrons. You can imagine how I feel about it, but I am in the Army now and there is nothing to do except make the best of it here." [20]

Hobey's so-called promotion, from his close friend and commanding officer Charley Biddle, had forced him to the sidelines yet again. This occasion nearly crushed Hobey's spirits. He was missing some of the most intense aerial combat of World War I. The St. Miehel and Verdun offensives were underway, and Hobey was relegated to making evening phone calls to Biddle, learning of both tragedy (the loss of three men, including Colonel Thaw's brother Blair) and triumph (eight Boche planes destroyed). [21] Those surreal calls must have been maddening for commanding officer Baker; so close to the action, yet so far.

Despite the outcome, Charley Biddle had every intention of getting his protégé to the front. "Hobey certainly had a run of the hardest kind of luck," said Biddle in his memoir. [22] The following is an entry lifted from Biddle's diary at the time:

He and [Richard] Mansell were recommended by me to take squadrons of their own, and each was given a squadron. Hobey came out ahead of Mansell, and was given the first to go. As bad luck would have it, Baker's squadron was not yet ready, while the other one that Mansell was given a week later was ready to go to the front. Now Mansell's squadron has been operating on the front for six weeks while Hobey is still in the rear. It's too bad, for Hobey is one of the very best, a very skillful pilot, and has all the nerve in the world, and is a thorough gentleman. He is one of the fairest, most straightforward fellows I know, and should make an excellent squadron commander, but he has struck rum luck from the start. I know how he frets in his present position and wishes he could be here at the front with us again. [23]

The 141st settled into their temporary quarters on August 30, but Hobey's baggage and bedding had been left in Paris. He alertly parlayed a two-day leave and wired Mimi to meet him. Blanketed by military red tape, he sensed the war slipping away, and feared his service might end with his chance at wartime glory wasted. On Saturday night, August 31, Hobey arrived in Paris on emotional tenterhooks. There was no sign of Mimi, so Baker dined alone at the Maurice Hotel. He then went to the theater and "felt lost," going home and crashing early. Sunday was another anxious day of waiting. He dropped by Mimi's apartment on Rue de Lille, but there was no sign and no word from her. Mimi's maid confirmed to Hobey that his telegram had long ago been forwarded to her at the front. [24]

Spirits sagging, Hobey had an uneventful lunch and another early supper. Still no word. Young aviator Barclay Warburton, a family friend from Philadelphia, was entertaining Sunday night in his Paris flat. Before heading over, Hobey made a 9 p.m. phone call to Mimi's apartment, with no answer. "I gave her up," said Hobey, who was battling the onset of heartache. [25]

Musician and soldier Jim Europe, a second lieutenant from the famed *Harlem Hellfighters* regiment, would be performing that night at Warburton's spacious apartment. When Lieutenant Europe wasn't fighting Germans, he and his band were turning out an exhilarating new form of music, the forerunner to American blues and jazz. Once Hobey arrived at Warburton's private concert, he found the innovative music to be a reprieve for his melancholy, as the tall black man banged out an early version of ragtime on the piano. Hobey was transformed by the rapid tempo and Europe's frenetic pounding of the keys. After the performance, Hobey made a point of connecting socially with Lieutenant Europe, who was a close acquaintance of Percy Pyne's. [26] Bringing up their popular mutual friend, and still glowing from the nouveau jazz performance, Hobey emerged from his funk, tapping into his nearly-forgotten joie de vivre.

They all went out to a wealthy Parisian's home for a bite to eat, enjoying themselves thoroughly before Hobey finally returned to the Maurice Hotel, his long day finally winding down after midnight. There at the front desk was an urgent message…from Mimi! "Come see me. No matter what time you get in." [27] Hobey sprinted over to Mimi's apartment, heart racing. All the emotional anguish he had felt that weekend was instantly turned around when he reunited with Mimi. Words from the heart poured out of Hobey, all reciprocated. Within minutes they had made the ultimate decision—they would go public with their engagement.

The first person Hobey notified was his father. "It is all fixed, *and we are engaged!* Don't quite understand how I put it across, but I did, and I know you will be glad. Please write Mimi and tell her how glad you are. She is so much what I have always wanted, that I feel all sort of safe and happy." [28]

How safe Mimi felt is undetermined. They spent that Monday shopping, and Hobey's next act was to seek Percy's help in liquidating a bond for the $500 needed to buy Mimi's ring. Hobey was nearly out of funds, engaged to a woman conditioned to boundless wealth. Hobey ignored that reality, lost in a 24-hour love-induced euphoria, coming on the heels of weeks of depression. The two lovers awoke from their sensual dream and departed first thing Tuesday morning: Mimi to the Compiegne hospital, and Hobey to the painstaking task of prepping his raw squadron for the final throes of the Great War.

In a complete turnabout, the love-struck officer finally welcomed publicity, as Hobey eagerly shared the joy of his engagement with all his pen pals. The sensational news soon went viral in the U.S. newspapers, and society queen Mimi Scott stole the headlines. "Mimi Scott Engaged" blared one newspaper, over the subheading "Popular Leader of Newport Set to be Bride of Lieutenant Baker, Aviation Corps." [29] The pragmatic Mimi Scott, described by Hobey as "very decided, with lots of brains," spent the next month taking inventory.

Hobey, meanwhile, spent September of 1918 focused on his mission, immersed in administering a crash course in flying to his young pups, as well as coordinating their new base in Toul. As the Allied casualties mounted, Hobey was forced to actually lend his young pilots to Biddle and Mansell to fly their aircrafts, while he desperately waited for his own. Biddle, Mansell and Rickenbacker all padded their deadly scoresheets, while Hobey was once again forced to the sidelines during the war's thrilling finale. In addition, he was stranded without ground transportation, and whatever synergetic passion he shared with Mimi was fading to black. For Baker, dark days had returned.

On September 25, Hobey reached out to Percy, a man whose affections for Hobey remained steadfast. "Mail has stopped, and even Mimi is lost to me," wrote Baker. "I have tried wiring her several times, but I don't believe any of them ever reached her. It is a horrible feeling to be so utterly away from everyone you love, and at times I get very depressed and blue. If I could only see Mimi more often, it would change everything." [30]

Probably not. While Hobey was putting heart and soul into the Allied war effort, Mimi was being courted by a new beau, Philander L. Cable, a wealthy diplomat based in Paris. In the oft-heartless game of love, the calculating Miss Scott had set a new course, one that did not include the financially strapped Captain Baker. The timing could not have been worse.

On October 12, Hobey answered his father's request for a description of Mimi, the woman the infirm Bobby Baker pre-

sumed would be his future daughter-in-law. Hobey continued to gush about Mimi, but he sensed trouble. "Oh! She is so
wonderful. Only a few inches shorter than I, broad shouldered
and yet gives the impression of slenderness. She is beautifully
graceful, which I love." Then in the same letter, Hobey appears
to sober up from his reverie. "She sort of worries me now, I have
not seen her in a month." [31]

A week later, Hobey writes his father again, having just
learned that his engagement was a mirage. "I think she is in love
with some man in Paris. It seems so queer, because she made
me feel so sure of her. We really had been engaged for about
five months, but I was anxious not to announce it until after the
war. I believe she honestly believed she loved me." Then Hobey
closed with a sarcastic line that revealed his delicate state: "I
sure am good when it comes to girls." [32]

It is hard to comprehend how crushing this must have been
to Hobey, the son who had never recovered from his mother's abandonment. Mimi Scott represented a woman's love, a
safe place to expose his fragile heart. Now that heart had been
dropped, and shattered.

From all accounts, Hobey did not wallow; he could not
afford to, there was still a war to be won. His promotion was
soon official—he was now a captain in the U.S. Army. Despite
rumors and predictions of an imminent German surrender,
Boche planes were still flying, and Hobey had finally received a
hangar full of his own to hunt them down. By mid-October he
had successfully trained a handful of pilots that he could trust
to ride shotgun with him on his sorties behind enemy lines.
When back on the ground, he returned to the one component
of his life that had never failed him—male sporting camaraderie. He had his loyal squadron paint orange tiger stripes on
their planes, as well as some radical artwork of a tiger ripping
at a Boche helmet with exposed claws. Hobey procured a foot-

ball, and in no time had his young charges engaged in games of touch whenever possible. Fired up, he dashed off a letter to his favorite Princeton wingman.

"It may be rah, rah, but I am having all the radiators painted orange and black, and a tiger's head for the squadron insignia," said Hobey in a note to Wendel Kuhn. "It will be damn pretty." [33]

Bolstered by regular flying missions and a fraternal lifestyle, Hobey's natural enthusiasm soon returned. Author and historian Charles Woolley remembered reading the journal of one of Hobey's young fliers, stating how popular Hobey had become with his men, playing football together during down time. "He was loved by all," said Woolley. "When these guys were scrimmaging, throwing the ball around, Hobey would join them. One diary said *Hobey Baker was playing touch with us and said 'Boy that fellow, (the diarist) he's played ball before!'* The diarist was all swelled up from that. So Hobey was a great asset from that perspective." [34]

Captain Baker maintained his positive disposition even when the fallout from his failed romance kept intruding into his mail call; his notifications of the breakup travelled much more slowly than the news of a celebrity engagement. "I keep getting letters of congratulations about Mimi," wrote Hobey to his father on October 29. "I will be glad when that's over. It's worse than when I was getting congratulations over all the Huns I hadn't brought down. It's damn unpleasant." [35]

Baker's personal issues seemed trivial compared to the human carnage that enveloped him daily. The day before he wrote about the Mimi Scott well-wishers, he went to a nearby evacuation hospital to see one of his injured fliers. "In the same ward was a man with a knee-cap gone," wrote Hobey to his father, "a man with one leg off and badly wounded, another with most of his insides out and so on. All of them laughing and joking, or trying to. I have never seen such spirit in my life, watching them made me want to burst out crying." [36]

Despite the mounting evidence that the Great War was in its twilight, Baker was intensely committed to the war effort, like a football scrub in a fresh uniform getting into a game with the outcome already decided. Charley Biddle was in Toul frequently in late October, now the commander of several squadrons, including the 141st. Hobey would dine with Biddle and other veterans of the massive September offenses, and listen wistfully as they recited their tales of multi-plane aerial combat. It ignited memories of his lone massive dogfight back in May, and his response was always the same. He did not mask his sentiments in that night's letter home. "I certainly would give up command of this squadron to have flown through one of those attacks. It must have been wonderful." [37]

Hobey had spent the vast majority of his war service in waiting: for planes, for capable men, for provisions and for a base itself; but now Hobey had finally positioned himself for the aerial war he had long dreamt about. His patience and dedicated supervision resulted in his commanding a competent air squadron for the last two weeks of the war. Hobey never got into the gigantic donnybrooks that had rewired him five months prior, but he engaged in small scraps nearly every day in the war's final throes.

On the last day of October, Hobey was flying apart from his group, protecting a five-plane patrol from a distance. He sensed an attack on a low flying Allied observation balloon, and sprinted down to the scene just as the balloon burst into flames. Baker spotted the perpetrator, a handsome Fokker biplane. He was hurrying back toward the safety of the German lines after committing the seemingly perfect crime. Hobey accelerated into the chase, turning a hit-and-run into a mano a mano pursuit, a classic knight's duel. His letter home that night read like an adventure novel for boys.

He got over a woods, and I lost him for a few valuable seconds, then picked him up as he shot across a road directly below me. I dove again and came out on his tail where I commenced firing at very close range. He pulled a climbing turn and came up over me. I saw the pilot look down and would recognize him if I saw him on the street we were so close. He was a beautiful pilot in a beautiful machine, a single seater with a black and white striped tail. I fired 150 rounds into him at close range. [38]

The German eventually crashed into the woods out of sight of Hobey, but as the eyewitness reports came in, it was soon confirmed—Baker had racked up his second official kill. This gentle man, hockey's most forgiving sportsman, had been hardened by the wartime deaths of friends and comrades, as well as a romance gone horribly wrong. Hobey was now a stone-cold killer, and woe be to the enemy pilot with Captain Baker on his tail.

Days later, it could just as easily have been Baker who was added to the immense World War I death toll. Firing from behind enemy lines, his gun's synchronicity with his propeller malfunctioned, and his bullets began chipping away at his own propeller. Miraculously, his gun jammed, preventing him from shooting out the propeller entirely. He somehow managed to limp home to the safety of his own lines. Ever since joining the Lafayette Escadrille in May, Hobey had survived countless moments with enemy guns streaming tracers into his own machine, living on the narrowest edge imaginable. This Princeton Tiger cat had a seemingly endless supply of lives.

Hobey concluded the war with another dramatic kill. He was a member of a five-man party that discovered a luckless German biplane distributing propaganda over the Allied lines. Captain Baker maneuvered his way underneath the enemy's soft underbelly, and poured in hundreds of bullets. "He suddenly rolled over on his back and went down," said Hobey. Baker and his patrol discovered that the second man, the observer, was already dead, falling out of his cockpit while upside down.

"We must have killed him with the first few bullets. He fell four thousand meters, that's two and half miles." [39] Any semblance of Hobey's sensitive empathy was long forgotten at this final stage in the war. He was making up for lost killing time.

Sharing in the action of the Great War's final fortnight generated mutual loyalty among Hobey and his young troops. "I am really very well pleased with the work of the squadron," wrote Baker. "We lost no men and have two Huns to our credit in two weeks of operating. I'm glad it is over, but I would not have minded a few more weeks to get this squadron at its height of efficiency." [40] To Captain Baker, however, leadership was secondary. He was a pursuit pilot, and remained hungry for action until the very end. What he did not say in his concluding letter was that he was desperate for more time to rack up two more kills, seeking that precious "Ace" status to complement his Croix de Guerre for bravery. His was an endless search for affirmation.

On the morning of the Armistice, Hobey spent hours flying solo on one final patrol, fighting through clouds until the visibility reached zero. He dropped down to ground level, but was once again blinded by fog. "Flying around like mad and just missing everything," wrote Hobey of his last act before the war shut down. "I finally put her into a field and stopped just short of some barbed wire." [41] He waited until the mist cleared before commencing on his lonely flight home. World War I, and with it Hobey's last defined purpose in life, had come to a frustrating close.

The SPAD aircraft whose engine cut out in midflight over Captain Baker's air field in Toul, France. (St. Paul's School)

CHAPTER THIRTEEN

The Crash of 1918

D espite the ache from missing out on his chance to become a pursuit pilot "Ace," Hobey remained a diligent squadron leader to the very end. He kept his Aerodrome in Toul in fine working order, and as captain, he quenched his thirst for flying whenever he chose. On November 21, he made a point of flying at low altitude over nearby Metz, observing first-hand the wreckage from the Huns. On his return, Hobey's engine inexplicably went dead. Knowing the Spad as well as he did, he merely glided to a safe landing on the side of a hill, a few kilometers away. He then had to commandeer an ambulance, and was forced to make two different stops before finding a phone to notify his base. Captain Baker needed assistance from several parties before finally arriving home late that night. The episode clearly embarrassed him. "I felt like a fool because I could not tell what the trouble was." [1] Hobey, by far the best flier in the squadron, limped home with wounded pride.

Once it became clear to Hobey that the war's end was inevitable, he allowed himself to fantasize about returning to the States. He may not have had a post-war career track in mind, but there is no doubt he longed for home. He made several entries to his father and Percy about his return, none more sentimental than the letter he penned to his father three days before the

Armistice. "To get back is Oh! such a wonderful thought. I just can't imagine the joy of walking into the house at Princeton and seeing you and [stepmother] Aunt Laura, Marie and Thornton. This peace talk has sort of brought it all home how much I want you, but I suppose I must put it out of my mind, since it is really a thought for some distant date." [2]

There is a long list of reasons why Hobey wanted to get back to the U.S. alive; the most persuasive deal with family. Thornton and Marie had a second child while Hobey was in France, naming him Hobart Amory Hare Baker. Hobey was delighted with the initial news, and even more so when Marie mailed him locks of his baby nephew's hair. [3]

Another factor, never stated in letters but evidenced from several other sources, is that Alfred Baker's physical condition was rapidly deteriorating. Rolf Bauhan, the man with whom Hobey toured Europe by motorcycle, noted that Hobey's dad was confined to a wheelchair during their final years together while students at Princeton [4], making the son all the more eager to see his dad while he still could. The elder Baker's disease was one of perpetual physical degeneration. This helps explain Hobey's patience and understanding for a father who repeatedly shared his son's war exploits with newspapermen, fueling stories that clearly aggravated him. Bauhan also noted that Hobey had written him, saying he was eager to get home to celebrate the end of the war together. [5]

The primary counter arguments, ones that imply suicide, were that Hobey had no career prospects, and that he was lovesick at the conclusion of the war. Granted, the fallout from Hobey's botched romance with Mimi Scott was indeed a social disaster. Baker was also irked by the fact that Scott continued writing him after the breakup. But while assessing Hobey's state of mind toward the end of his life, his love of family trumps any heartache he may have felt due to his failed relationship.

And finally, Hobey was terribly eager to reconnect with his

best friend and trusted confidante Percy Pyne. In a November 16 letter, his last on record to Percy, he said that he "hated the idea of being killed right at the finish." [6]

Even though Hobey was willing to stay in France as long as his country required, the November 16 letter to Percy revealed his true sentiments. "I am afraid being in the second Army it is going to be a long weary wait, I won't see home in a year or more, *unless you with all your influential friends can do something for me.*" [Emphasis added by author.] [7] Hobey's last sentence was not merely a throwaway line to his best friend. Percy Pyne was a powerful man in both New York and Washington, currently in his second year managing the finances for the Army's Bureau of Defense.

Not coincidentally, Hobey received his orders to return home a month later, leapfrogging thousands of places in line in the process. He was now scheduled to ship out on December 22, 1918, his journey to begin on the 8 p.m. train to Paris the night before. Percy's fingerprints were all over those orders.

Hobey's November 16 letter to Percy included some salient news in addition to the plea to facilitate his early exit from France. Baker mentioned a character who will forever be linked to Hobey's saga. The ubiquitous Donald "Heff" Herring had returned, as if Baker's screenwriter inserted this familiar figure into the story as a human thread to help the audience stitch yet another moment of drama into the quilt of Hobey's life. "Heff Herring from Princeton has showed up here as Group Armament Officer," writes Hobey, "and I was damn glad to see him." [8]

For followers of Hobey Baker, we are all damn glad to see him. Herring is the ideal man—Hobey's former preceptor and assistant football coach—to serve as the witness who might make sense of the tragic conclusion to Baker's life. As it happened, Herring was alongside Baker in Toul when the captain received his orders to return home in late December. "Hobey thought it was his duty to stay with the squadron," wrote Herring. "So against my advice, he took the unusual step of making a personal request to Colonel Lahm, commanding officer of second Army Air Service, to ask for a change in orders." [9] Baker's quixotic quest to have his orders home rescinded set the scene for Hobey's farewell act.

Captain Baker's final day started in a pre-dawn rush. Early Saturday morning, December 21, Hobey commandeered both a combination motorcycle and driver Howard Nieland, and together they putted off to Paris while most of the squadron slept. The orders to return to the United States created mixed feelings in Hobey: he longed to get home from a personal standpoint, but he awoke with misgivings. He felt like he would be abandoning his squadron if he returned home months before them, so he sought an immediate audience with Colonel Frank Lahm to nix them, on a Saturday no less. No sooner had Hobey tracked down the Colonel in Paris than he was immediately sent back to Toul, his orders to return home emphatically confirmed. Due to all the fawning newspaper accounts published on both sides of the Atlantic, Hobey was one of America's best-known soldiers. This war hero was coming home, ASAP.

Despite a light rain, it was a giddy Captain Baker who returned to the base around 11 a.m. His fellow officers knew something was awry when driver Nieland was in the sidecar, feet up, smoking a cigar. Hobey burst into the officers' quarters, and according to Davies, "ran around the room swishing his orders under their envious faces." [10] This is a side of Hobey never described before. The Hobey Baker Collection contains over 200 letters from him during World War I, and there are hundreds of anecdotes amassed by Davies and nephew Henry Baker, but none of them ever described Hobey acting with such inelegance. Clearly he was out of sorts, the reality of his imminent departure kicking in, and being met with internal resistance. Leaving the squadron would be abandoning his mates and his new home, one he had painstakingly built atop a foundation of fraternal camaraderie. The 141st Aero Squadron had an aura reminiscent of Hobey's school days, where you competed and fought and threw the ball around with chums in team colors, safe from the heartache of uncaring women. Baker was now just hours away from a train ride that would forever separate him from the emotional safety of his loyal squadron. The orders he held in his hands triggered an internal sense of helplessness, a feeling that his life was spinning out of control.

In terms of fighting off insecurity, action sports had always been Hobey's buffer, whether it was football, hockey or flying. His unspoken fear of abandonment, first experienced as a child in Philadelphia, had continued to grow. Efforts to insulate him, first at prep school, then college, continuing through his time at the Pyne mansions and country clubs, and finally here in Toul, were only temporary. As Baker frenetically hopped around the officer's quarters, the thought of flying, and the instant relief it would provide, struck him, and struck him hard.

High functioning adults operate in logical sequence: intentional thoughts become spoken words, and those words lead to action. At this crucial time and place, Hobey was desperate for action. With the full attention of the room, the commanding officer made an announcement that began a fatal sequence of events: Hobey was going to take "one last flight in the old Spad."[11] The room, which only moments before had been filled with happy scenes of good natured ribbing and one-upsmanship, immediately went stone cold. To a man, everyone knew that it was more dumb luck than skill that they were still alive and sipping cognac. Just as many fliers died from training accidents on their own turf as they did in battle. Taking a final flight was foolish at best, a death wish at worst.

Soon the room echoed with loud protests, but Baker would have none of it—he was commanding officer and his word was final. The colonels and majors in Paris might have been able to order him home, but here in his own squadron, there was no one to tell the Captain what he could or could not do. At that moment, Hobey wanted to fly. More than anything else, he needed to be airborne.

Colonel Biddle, who outranked Hobey, would have ordered Baker to stand down, and prevented his friend from taking that last flight, lest it be exactly that. But Biddle had shipped home three weeks earlier. Hobey's former professor, Heff Herring, seven years his elder and a man who held sway over Baker's actions many times in his life, attempted to do just that. But Herring no longer had power over his former charge. Baker brushed aside Herring and headed to the hangar, in search of his trusty old Spad Number 2; shouts of protest in his wake.

As Hobey marched defiantly into the hangar, an unnamed mechanic greeted Baker with Hitchcockian timing, and impact. "Captain Baker, sir, Number 7 is ready for flight test." [12] This was a plane whose carburetor had recently failed in mid-flight, putting a scare into one of Captain Baker's young pilots. The mechanic had switched out the wonky Claudel carburetor and replaced it with an untested Zenith.

Once Hobey learned that he was flying Spad Number 7, the one that had put his loyal subordinate in jeopardy, his quest to get airborne took on a whole new meaning. No longer was it about one last joy ride, it was now about honor and duty. Whatever chance his outranked squadron had of talking him out of this fool's errand had now vanished.

"As long as I am commander of this squadron, it is my duty that no one risks his life after I am gone." The words echoed like an epitaph, "...*after I am gone.*" [13] One insubordinate soldier wheeled out Hobey's old Spad Number 2, but Hobey dismissed it. [14] The mechanic, now following his captain's orders, prepped Spad Number 7 for its final mission. Herring recalled those moments in vivid detail. "Hobey ordered Number 7 to be rolled out, and climbed into the cockpit." [15]

Herring knew only too well of Hobey's penchant for aerial stunts, how he relished tempting the fates while airborne. He urgently rushed out for a final conversation with his one-time protégé. "The sergeant spun the prop, the motor caught," said Herring. "While it was warming up, Hobey gave me his promise once more that he would fly straight out to Pont-a-Mousson and back, a 40-mile trip, and land without acrobatics." [16] It was a broken promise.

Human memory can function with supreme efficiency when scorched by intense emotion. Thirty-nine years after Herring witnessed the destruction of his beautiful friend, he was able to record the episode in glaring detail.

> *With the motor thoroughly warmed up, Hobey headed into the wind. After becoming airborne, he held the nose down and gunned the Hispano motor up to 2200 revs, the plane scarcely twenty feet off the ground. With the motor delivering full power, he suddenly pulled up in a right chandelle, the most nearly vertical climb that planes of that day could make. He levelled off at a hundred meters, and headed toward the northeast corner of the field. Hobey had flown perhaps a quarter of a mile after levelling off, and was approaching the little square of trees and barn. Just here, at the worst possible place and fraction of time, his motor cut out. The sergeant and I started to run.* [17]

At the time of his motor failing, Hobey was pointed toward the northeast border of the rectangular air field, directly toward a "dense growth of sturdy saplings surrounding a huge stone barn." Herring realized his friend was in double jeopardy.

> *[Hobey] Quite possibly could have held the Spad's nose up long enough to clear the telegraph wires and stone barracks and land in the ploughed land behind. He would have washed out the plane, but he might have got out*

without serious injury to himself. I had seen crashes on
hard ground where the plane was demolished, and the
pilot walked away with not even a bloody nose. As I ran, I
prayed it might happen just one more time. [18]

Despite the prayers, Herring knew better. In the recounting
of this tragic story, Herring demonstrates why he was the perfect witness: not only because of his physical vantage point, but
also because he knew the pilot better than anyone else on Gen-
goult Field. Here at the crucial juncture of Hobey's fatal flight,
storytellers must fill in the blanks, because Hobey did not live
to explain his reasoning. Herring still sensed Hobey's humiliation from washing out his plane on November 21, how his
protégé "felt like a fool" when he returned from Metz. In this
final flight, with his entire crew as his rapt audience, Hobey had
two options: to "wash out" his plane once again, or to attempt an
acrobatic high-risk escape. The latter course had been pounded
into his DNA since his childhood in Philadelphia. Herring continued the tragic play-by-play.

The sergeant and I knew what he was thinking. He was
not only commanding officer, he was the oldest and best
pilot in his squadron. He did not want to wash out his
ship, especially this one, on his last flight. In a fraction of
a second he had to make the decision. He chose to attempt
that which every good pilot has felt himself compelled to
choose at some crisis, namely, to risk 'Getting Back on the
Field.' [19]

This is the moment in time that has been debated for a century: Hobey choosing not to glide into a roughed-up landing,
but instead, turning back to the field with a dead engine. There is
a vital chapter in Hobey's flight history that factors into his fatal
decision to reverse field. While on patrol seven months earlier
in Dunkirk, Baker discovered that the throttle on his new Spad
was stuck wide open, and he had to kill the engine, forced to

land his machine with no power. This is what Hobey wrote to his father the night of May 27, 1918. "I had never brought a Spad down before without motor and with the propeller stopped. The result was I misjudged the field and fell short. I learned something about bringing a Spad down with a dead motor. They are very heavy and lose height remarkably fast." [20]

In light of that fact, Hobey's decision to turn back to the field may not have been so confounding after all. As described vividly by Herring, Hobey's dead-weight Spad was pointed towards telegraph wires, stone barracks, and a grove of trees. Baker knew from experience that due to the weight of his machine, he was heading toward a potentially disastrous crash when he chose to make his fatal turn. Herring continues.

He made a right turn, lost flying speed, and began to fall off on a wing. He then did the only thing that might possibly have saved him had he had just a little more altitude— he turned the nose straight down.

Maybe another hundred feet of altitude might have saved him. About 90 feet from the ground the plane started to spin. My legs gave way as I ran. I had witnessed fatal crashes before, some of them by friends to whom I had been talking just before they took off. This was different— and worse.

The first to reach the crash were three officers who were walking along the entrance road in front of the stone barracks. Hobey's right foot was caught in the wire loop of the rudder bar, and it took time to work it loose. He died as we lifted him out of the plane. The engine was buried several feet in the soft ground. [21]

Save once, I never saw Hobey's face without the appearance of life in it, and that once was the moment he died in my arms. [22]

Mere minutes earlier, Hobey Baker had been full of manic

joy, prancing around the officers' quarters with orders in hand, his heart filled with laughter. Now he was inert, a five-inch gash on the right side of his forehead. This epic athlete, a hauntingly beautiful man who lived above the clouds with a song on his lips, was now relegated to history. Hobart Amory Hare Baker died December 21, 1918 at 11:55 a.m. local time, his orders home inside his jacket. He perished three weeks before his 27th birthday.

The squadron hastily arranged Baker's burial service for the following day, and Lieutenant Inglehart wired the terrible bulletin back home to Percy Pyne, who now shouldered the obligation to notify next of kin with the shocking news. On December 22, the day Hobey was scheduled to sail home, he was buried on the outskirts of Toul at the American military cemetery. He was laid to rest next to another romantic figure, Lafayette Escadrille flying ace Raoul Lufbery. Herring and Gil Winant, another Princeton man, served as the first pall bearers. As Hobey was lowered into the ground, a soprano soloed the pure notes from a haunting Episcopal hymn.

Nearer my God to Thee,
Or, if on Joyful wing,
Caught up to meet my King,
Swiftly I'll fly. [23]

Not everyone on the field that day comprehended Hobey's radical decision to turn back to the field on that final flight. Eyewitness Lieutenant Edward C. Olds (Princeton, '09) shared his account with the *New York Times*. "It has cast a cloud over the Second Army Air Service, where he was very well-known and liked by officers and men." Olds opined that Baker might have saved his life had he not tried to reverse course in an attempt to return to the Toul aerodrome. [24] It is unlikely that Lieutenant

Olds knew how an airborne Spad performed without power as well as his Captain did.

Although Baker had always been a loyal soldier, he had also been a solo artist his entire life. His tendency to take enormous risks were ingrained from an early age. Those quick-trigger impulses led to free-lancing behind enemy lines, and often kept him alive during his career as a pursuit pilot, dodging, spinning and looping instantaneously. Nothing would be more appropriate for Hobey Baker, the athlete, than to "reverse field" when faced with adversity in the midst of a sortie. Whether it be football, hockey or flying, performing a high-speed about-face when confronted by danger was Baker's tried and true solution. That fact, coupled with the pride of being his squadron's top-ranking officer, made Hobey's life-and-death decision to head back to the field a logical one from his perspective, despite its fatal outcome.

Within a week, American newspapers published solemn and reverential obituaries about Baker, mourning one of America's all-time great athletes and sportsmen. Rolf Bauhan, Hobey's roommate at Princeton his senior year, was headed into the Nassau Club dining room for coffee, two days after Christmas. "I came down to breakfast and picked up my mail," said Bauhan, "including a letter from Hobey. When I sat down to read the morning paper, here was the story of Hobey's death." [25]

'HOBEY' BAKER DIES IN FALL OF AIRPLANE was the headline in that morning's *New York Times*. [26] It took Bauhan several minutes to compose himself, digesting the tragic news of the loss of a dear friend, with the letter from the same man in his hands. He later described the contents of that note from France. "I had a letter from Hobey in anticipation of his coming back and our having a celebration together." [27] Their friendship, and the stunning news of Baker's death, had a lasting impact on Bauhan. Over a decade later he named his second son Hobart Baker Bauhan.

Some newspapermen conjured up explosive stories follow-ing Captain Baker's sensational death, with scandalous implica-tions—suicide. The fact that their storyline may have conflicted with the facts from Toul did not stem the tide. The controversy was fueled by the timing of a parallel news flash that dovetailed perfectly with Hobey's death: the wedding of Mimi Scott to embassy man Philander Cable. One New York paper included both items in the same December 28 headline:

CAPT. HOBEY BAKER MET HIS DEATH
IN FALL OF 2000 FEET

Football and Hockey Star's Former Fiancé Reported
Married in Paris [28]

National sports columnist O.T. Gurnee connected the dots, and drew a sensational, if not corroborated, conclusion. In his popular Sunday column, Gurnee printed what had been rumored for months. "He had been engaged to a girl in the States, and it was whispered that her marriage announcement was received the morning he hopped off for the last time. If ever a man deliberately 'nosed down,' and gave his ship the gun with the fullest intention of 'going west' on the wing, that man was Hobey Baker." [29] As was the case during his life, dubious news-paper accounts dogged Hobey, even after he was dead and gone.

Nearly a full year after Hobey's death, Heff Herring finally received his orders home. He carefully gathered Hobey's per-sonal effects, including his medals and a cache of letters, and placed them in a briefcase, which he carried on his person to la gare d'Orleans train station. He placed the satchel between his legs while purchasing his ticket for Paris, when "a daring thief stole my briefcase from between my feet." [30] Herring acted quickly, enlisting local and military police, even offering rewards for the case, all to no avail. Despondent, Herring returned to Princeton with nothing for Baker's grieving family but the story of his death.

Hobey and Princeton roommate Rolf Bauhan in Europe on their 1914 motorcycle tour. After learning of Baker's death, Bauhan named his son Hobey Baker Bauhan. (St. Paul's School)

HOBEYQUEST:
THE GHOST OF HOBEY

Biographer John Davies asserted that Hobey spent all four of his Princeton years living above Renwick's restaurant in a large apartment with half a dozen of his St. Paul's chums. Long-term residents of Princeton, however, know differently. Toward the end of Hobey's tenure at Ol' Nassau, he moved into a carriage house near Lake Carnegie. A close friend of mine is a neighbor of the current owner of the estate, and agreed to introduce me.

During one of my Princeton visits in 2015, the name of the owner Hobey's former abode struck me—Jamie *Herring*! How could Jamie *not* be related to the Herring from Baker's era? After all, "Heff" Herring was a ubiquitous character in Hobey's saga: he was Baker's advisor at Princeton and the man who held Hobey when he took his last breath. It was time to pay a visit to the Herring/Hobey house.

Prior to a 2015 Princeton hockey game, I detoured west to Castle Howard Court and rang the bell unannounced. Jamie Herring wasn't in, but his wife was. Although polite, Kathy Herring did not share my enthusiasm for this quest. I could tell this was not the time for a tour of Hobey's quarters, but I was determined to make the Herring connection. Kathy firmly denied her husband was related to Princeton professor Donald Herring. She insisted that Jamie's family tree came from a different Herring branch. That fact was later confirmed in a follow-up call to Jamie. Dripping with proverbial cold water, I saw myself out from the Herring estate.

It wasn't until 2018 that I finally connected with Jamie to get my tour of Hobey's carriage house. I soon discovered that this was much more than off-campus living for Hobey and his classmates; this was father Alfred Baker's final resting spot, the estate that he and his second wife Laura purchased and moved into in

1913. I spent nearly an hour touring the "House of Baker," gazing at the same artwork and murals that Hobey and his father had viewed, testing the keyboard of the now-defunct grand organ in Hobey's quarters, and peeking into Laura Baker's art studio that had been constructed in the summer of 1914. It was an exquisite visit, one that not only connected historic dots, but one that gave me a chance to step into Hobey's personal living space. And then Herring shared a story that suspended belief.

In the early 2000's, the Herrings brought over an au pair from South Africa named Deloshny Pilay, an Indian woman who had never before set foot in the United States. She was given Hobey's old quarters as her living space. On one of her first nights on the job, she woke the Herrings with her shrieks from the other side of the house. Jamie dashed over to investigate. He found Pilay cowering under her blankets.

"I asked her what was wrong," recalled Herring. "A man was staring at me!" said the shaken foreigner, her beddings pulled up just below her eyes. Deloshny had seen someone at the foot of her bed, covered herself and began shrieking. When she summoned the courage for a second glance, he was still there. Herring asked for a description of what turned out to be an apparition. "She said the man wore a leather hood, and a pair of goggles." It was essentially a World War I flying uniform. Jamie stated that Pilay had no clue as to the history of the house or its inhabitants. She worked one more year for the Herring family.

U.S. Army Captain Hobey Baker. (Getty Images)

CHAPTER FOURTEEN

For the Love of Hobey

On the first Wednesday of February, 1919, five weeks after Hobey's death, Princeton University held a service for its beloved Tiger. It was staged at Trinity Episcopal Church, the spiritual homestead of the Baker clan, where Hobey's great uncle Alfred had been the rector for 48 years. The Princeton community packed the stone church on the corner of Stockton Street and Bayard Lane, filled with recognizable athletes, financiers, and a heartsick Percy Pyne. Hobey's father Alfred, infirm with less than two years to live, was pushed in his wheelchair by his second wife Laura. His surviving son Thornton, soon to be an honorary member of the class of 1913, followed behind Alfred, accompanied by his wife Marie and their two children, Bobbie and 14-month-old toddler Hobey Baker II. Now a balding 28-year-old, Thornton paused outside the church to gaze at the enormous pine tree he and younger brother Hobey had scaled in their innocent youth.

Three clergymen relatives of Hobey performed the service, and Princeton president John Hibben, a former Presbyterian minister, delivered the address. "Ever since he entered the University, he has been the pride of Princeton," said Hibben, [1] "He lived with a divine disregard for his own safety." [2] The Princeton congregation nodded knowingly.

Pyne was the president of Princeton's class of 1903 at the time of Hobey's death, and wielded his considerable power at the University to help preserve his best friend's legacy. As the first person notified of Hobey's death, Pyne went to work immediately, starting with the unpleasant task of notifying next of kin. He then created a $10,000 scholarship in Hobey's name, followed by a much larger undertaking. No university in the country had its own hockey facility at the time—Yale and Princeton played at St. Nick's Arena, Harvard's Crimson skated at Boston Arena. Percy envisioned a world class rink on the Princeton campus in Hobey's name, and Pyne realized his dream in record time. With sentiment for Hobey running high, Percy solicited funds from every college athlete who competed with or against Baker, the men of Yale and Harvard in particular. In just over one year, Pyne raised a quarter of a million dollars (three million in 2018 dollars) from 1,537 individuals across 39 colleges. Other than Princeton, Harvard led the way with 172 donors; Yale registered 90. [3]

Baker Memorial Rink is a monument to Hobey's athletic triumvirate: Harvard, Yale, and Princeton, the Holy Trinity of Ivy league sports. The rink was constructed in gothic style with its high ceilings and stone arches, nestled into the southwest end of the Princeton campus. The hockey cathedral hosted its first game on January 5, 1922, with Princeton taking on St. Nick's. Nearly a century later it remains the home of the Tigers men's and women's varsity teams. When visiting Baker rink, fans of Hobey Baker can enter via a seldom used gate on the west side of the arena. A small set of stairs leads to a pair of heavy oak doors, framed by a pointed stone arch. If one looks carefully, the name "Hobart A. H. Baker" is visible on the left-hand side of the entrance, etched into the stone. Stepping through the arch, one finds oneself in a museum-like exhibit devoted to Hobey, with his original skates under glass, a large oil portrait of Captain

Baker in his Army uniform, and the 40-pound Hobey Baker Award.

Every nook, cranny and staircase of Baker Rink's north end zone is filled with aging images of Princeton hockey greats: John Cook; 1979 captain and Hollywood mogul David E. Kelley; and unsmiling portraits of Hobey in black and white. The 141st Aero Squadron and the class of 1914 are also honored, but nowhere in the entire building is a mention of the driving force who made it all possible, Percy Rivington Pyne 2nd.

After Hobey's death, his mother resurfaced in real estate records, remarried as Mary Pemberton Van Shutts. Hobey's parents were ordered to divide up their son's Bucks County farmhouse. On October 19, 1919, Alfred "Bobby" Baker, in the last year of his life, deeded his one-half share of the farmhouse to ex-wife Mary for one dollar. [4] Whatever animus the two parents once had for each other had apparently dissolved.

When the suffering Bobby Baker finally passed in November of 1920, Mary began orchestrating the return of Hobey's body to the U.S. for its proper burial. The U.S. government was returning fallen soldiers to families post World War I, but not on a timely basis. In a May 1921 letter, Mary reveals that she is expecting Hobey's body to arrive stateside in a few months. [5]

On July 14, 1921, a hot and humid Thursday afternoon in downtown Philadelphia, a large train bearing United States Army markings pulled into the city's Reading Terminal. Dozens of "war mothers" gathered on the platform to greet their fallen sons on the arriving train, Mary Van Shutts among them. Twenty-six bodies arrived that day, including that of Captain Hobart Amory Hare Baker. His casket, draped in an American flag, was loaded onto a caisson and drawn by horses through downtown

Philadelphia. A lone military officer attended the casket for its short trip to the local undertaker. [6]

At noon the following Tuesday, Hobey was laid to rest at the West Laurel Hill Cemetery in Bala Cynwyd. It was a proper military funeral, attended by a large contingent of Hobey's surrogate family from St. Paul's. That one institution lost a total of 48 men in the Great War, a deadly by-product of noblesse oblige. [7] Reverend Floyd Tompkins, a giant within Philadelphia's Episcopal community, conducted the service. During his eulogy, he referred to Captain Baker as "A fine sample of American manhood." [8] Following his words, three volleys were fired over the grave by four wounded veterans from the 109th infantry, and taps were sounded.

The accompanying photo in the *Philadelphia Enquirer* shows four civilians at the foot of the grave while the volleys of shots were fired. Mother Mary is next to a man in uniform, and standing next to them is Thornton and his wife Marie. A fifth person, an unidentified tall woman, stands next to Marie.

Hobey's Philadelphia burial was Mary Van Shutt's special tribute to the son she barely knew. It was her first chance to meet the St. Paul's community that had raised Hobey in her absence, including Walter Gearty and Thomas Emery Posts of the American Legion, and several other of Hobey's friends from St. Paul's. Despite the U.S. Army paying for Hobey's return to the States, the funeral and Hobey's plot required an outlay of cash she did not have. Financial assistance most likely came from Percy Pyne, the one person in Hobey's life who repeatedly visited Mary while Hobey was fighting the Germans overseas.

A prominent headstone was placed at Hobey's grave eight months after the funeral. [9] It is engraved with a beautiful, yet haunting poem, one that captures the essence of the fallen hero:

> *You who seemed winged, even as a lad,*
> *With that swift look of those who know the sky,*
> *It was no blundering fate that stooped and bade*

You break your wings, and fall to the earth and die.
I think one day you may have flown too high,
So that Immortals saw you and were glad,
Watching the beauty of your spirits flame,
Until they loved and called you, and you came

Where Mary found this verse remained a mystery to the public for nearly a century; three books and *Sports Illustrated* all labeled it anonymous. But every crafted line in the poem resonated with Hobey's spirit during his time on and above earth. The unsolved riddle of that poem stoked the intellectual curiosity of attorney J.P. Archer, who in 2014, used all of his considerable training and passion to try and unveil the author of the tombstone's verse. He spent a year chasing a bevy of tantalizing clues, many of which resulted in dead ends, before his sweat equity paid off. Archer's findings were eventually published in an essay for the *Princeton Alumni Weekly* after he discovered that the verse was written by a female writer whose pen name was "Amory Hare." [10] Her real name was Mary Amory Hare, Hobey's elder first cousin from Philadelphia, the same woman who helped raise him during his turbulent childhood.

Mary Hare knew precisely of what she wrote when she penned, *"You who seemed winged, even as a lad."* She had seen her cousin flying from tree branches in her back yard while growing up together in Philadelphia. Mary Van Shutts, Hobey's mother, had immortalized her son by using her niece's verse on Hobey's tombstone. Based on Archer's revelation, there is little doubt that the unidentified fifth person in the newspaper photo from the Philadelphia funeral was Mary Amory Hare, Hobey's loving older cousin. The headstone with its poignant poem was a pièce de résistance from the Philadelphia Pembertons, one never acknowledged by John Davies or anyone else in the Baker-dominated Princeton community. Remarkably, Mary Amory Hare's ode to cousin Hobey was first published in an essay for the *Princeton Alumni Weekly* (PAW) in 1919, only months after

Hobey's death. [11] Yet Davies, PAW's long-time editor, never mentioned the author, leaving it as a century-old mystery.

Of the three memorials to Hobey Baker—Toul, Princeton and Philadelphia—the latter was the one with the unmistakable stamp of Hobey's mom, one in which Mary provided both a timeless verse and a permanent resting spot for the American Icarus. For reasons still to be determined, Hobey's mom was absent from his life growing up, but she was an undisputable shining star after his death.

CHAPTER FIFTEEN

Suicide? The Great Debate

In 1991, the best writer in sports' best magazine wrote his best piece: Ron Fimrite's "A Flame That Burned Too Brightly," the story of Hobey Baker, published by *Sports Illustrated* on March 18. Just like the John Davies biography on Hobey from a generation prior, Fimrite's masterpiece ignited the passions of a brand-new legion of Hobey enthusiasts. The kicker in the S.I. piece was Fimrite's farewell statement: "…Hobey's death was not entirely accidental." [1]

It echoed Davies' reporting back in 1966: "The rumor of his suicide persists to this day, discussed by all aficionados of the Baker legend." [2]

The conclusion to Hobey's life is the element that leaves so many of us guessing. It is the romantic death of a chivalrous knight, the bookend to a tragic fairy tale, the James Dean of World War I. For those of us caught up in the history of Hobey, it is a question worth careful examination.

Octogenarian Stan Fischler is the quintessential hockey historian and author, who happens to live three miles north of the former site of Saint Nicholas Arena in Manhattan. He has a salient theory about Hobey's death. "That flight was a chance-taking thing, that he could beat it," said Fischler. "Also, the fact that if he couldn't beat it, then this is the way he wanted to go." [3]

Sports historian Stephen Hardy has long considered the fate of Hobey Baker, and he cannot rule out suicide, based on Hobey having no viable plans once he returned to the States. "Maybe… maybe…" and then Hardy's voice trails off. [4]

The end of Hobey's life is a riddle, and there is no consensus among the serious students of Hobey Baker. We have much of the same material, yet there are wide ranging manifestations. I introduced author Richard Stiles Greeley to the Baker Collection at Mudd Manuscript Library in 2013 and showed him the same letters I had long studied. Richard believed that Hobey was eager to return home in December 1918; I originally thought the opposite. Greely appeared to be naively ignoring the mountain of circumstantial evidence: with no career prospects and a broken heart, Hobey bucked orders to go home; his in-flight decision to reverse field and point the nose of his plane into the ground made it obvious to me that he intentionally ended his own life. Obvious for the time being, anyway.

Biographer Emil Salvini simply punted. Rather than make a statement as to how Hobey died, Salvini penned two final chapters to Baker's life: one an accident, and the other a suicide. Clearly, there is wide room for interpretation.

1960 Yale hockey captain Bruce Smith has been immersed in Hobey's story since discovering his romantic tale while playing at Yale. In 2017, Smith teamed up with Princeton grad Rick Sloane to complete a second screenplay on Hobey, "a more romantic version," albeit with a sad ending. "I can't bring myself to believing Hobey committed suicide," said Smith, pausing as he wrestled with the issue, and then considering the unthinkable. "Hobey did not have any plans after the war. Hockey had changed, and he wasn't going back to Wall Street." [5]

Paul Lally, the producer and writer of the Hobey video documentary *Golden,* spent a year immersed in Baker's story, and he happens to be an amateur pilot. He remains incredulous over Baker's choices while airborne in that final flight. "Rule one, if you take off and you have an engine failure, you *never* turn back to the field, no matter what," said Lally. He then tried to put himself into Baker's head, and mitigate the horrendous outcome. "The guy loved to fly, man, it was like a rush, I know what it's like. He miscalculated his air speed and his altitude, and God knows it was his last flight. I think his mind was thinking about going home and he miscalculated, fell off on a wing and crashed. Did he do it on purpose? Nah, I don't think so." [6] Lally is not convincing.

World War I flying author and an expert of the genre, Charles Woolley, literally shook his head as he considered Hobey's fatal last flight. "Instead of staying on a straight course, and bringing it down, Hobey turned back to the field, which is something no one ever would do," said Woolley. "Even a green pilot wouldn't have done that. It's always been somewhat questionable about what he was thinking about when he crashed." [7]

After World War I, several sportswriters—aware of Mimi Scott's rejection of Hobey before his death—jumped to the conclusion that Hobey had indeed committed suicide, infuriating Hobey's military peers. Heff Herring's detailed description of Hobey's fatal flight was published in the *Princeton Alumni Weekly* on November 1, 1957. Herring had a specific agenda when he penned that account for PAW.

"I wrote that letter once and for all to scotch the rumor that Hobey committed suicide because Mimi Scott had broken her engagement to him," said Herring. "This is a widely published lie, made up by some damned reporter at the time and widely circulated and believed. I knew a lot of pilots in 1917–18, and I never knew any who would have committed suicide." [8]

There were other members of Hobey's prep network that defended their Ivy League icon. "There is no basis for the assertion that Hobey might have committed suicide," wrote classmate Rolf Bauhan. "My brother in law, Julian Lathrop, Harvard '16, was at the field when Hobe died and in talking with him he observed that no such comment would have any merit." [9] Another Princeton classmate, Holbrook Cushman, spent two months of World War I with Baker, flight training with him in Issoudun in November and December of 1917. There was no doubt in Cushman's mind about what went down in Toul that fateful day. "Don't believe the nonsense about the intentional bad turn on his last flight," said Cushman. "I spent much time in Spads, when his Hispano motor cut out, there was nothing he or anyone else could do without altitude, and he didn't have altitude. This from the mouths of pilots that saw him fall that day at Toul." [10]

But according to eyewitness Lieutenant Edward Olds, another loyal Princeton man, there was plenty Hobey could have done to save his own life that day, and he wrote exactly that to the New York Times.

There is a legal pad full of evidence that makes a Hobey suicide plausible, especially all those letters from France in which Hobey appears to fantasize about death by air. His statement, "There couldn't be a nicer way to die…pleasant, quick and sure," turned out to be just that. Adding to that list is the fact that on December 21 Hobey's heart was still freshly bruised by Mimi, and that he was glum about his career prospects back in the U.S. The entire docket makes a reasonable, even compelling, case that Hobey did the unimaginable.

Ironically, when Hobey learned that his Princeton chum Gil Winant was heartsick over a breakup in the early stages of his World War I flying tour, Hobey wrote his father the following: "I suppose if Gil has a crash, Louise (his former lover) will think he is committing suicide because of her, but a crash is apt to come to anyone." [11]

Arguably the most powerful intellect to enter the debate is Oxford and Harvard Law product J.P. Archer, who has spent years examining the Baker collection at Princeton. "I haven't seen any evidence that makes suicide more likely than accident," writes Archer, who regrets that there are no Hobey letters written immediately prior to the crash. "The next most valuable evidence would be others' accounts of Hobey's mindset at the time, and we do have a few of those. None of them indicates any despondency or other mental or emotional difficulty.

"Hobey's decision to turn the plane is curious, I admit," continues Archer. "We won't ever know for sure exactly why he did it. But, all things considered, I'm willing to believe that it was most likely a combination of poor judgement, hubris, a lifelong tolerance-appetite for risk, and a wish to avoid the embarrassment of a crash landing off the field." [12]

Documents are often the most compelling evidence when trying to settle a debate. It was only after several return visits to Mudd Library—subsequent to my 2014 meetings with Greeley—that I did an about-face on Baker's death. There were three critical letters written by Hobey in 1918 that persuaded me to change my position to one of accident, and not suicide: 1) November 21, Hobey washed out his plane in Metz and returned to the base, saying he "felt like a fool;" 2) November 8, Hobey tells his ailing father what joy it would be to see the family back at Princeton, including his baby nephew and namesake Hobey II; and 3) May 27, Hobey describes how he learned the hard way how heavy the Spad aircraft is, how fast they descend without power. Based on those three elements: longing to return home to family, the still painful embarrassment of washing out his plane, and the very real possibility that gliding to a landing could have led to a disastrous collision, Hobey's choice to turn back is not only plausible, but conclusive.

When John Davies was poised to go to print with the official Baker biography in 1966, the galleys were shared with certain Princeton alums, including former U.S. Army major Charles Biddle, Hobey's World War I roommate and flying mentor.

Biddle began a furious letter-writing campaign, insisting that Davies' book scrub any mention of Baker's suicide.

On June 24, 1966, the 76-year-old Biddle wrote Davies in a last-ditch attempt to finally set the record straight. Biddle was a world class litigator at the time, still practicing law at his firm Drinker, Biddle and Reath in Philadelphia. Biddle knew the Toul airfield intimately from his final two months of the war, as did Hobey, the pilot whom he literally took under his wing. Biddle, fittingly, gets the last word.

> As anyone who knew Baker well should know, he was not the kind of man who would deliberately end his own life. While I was not there at the time of the accident, I have talked to numerous men who were there and saw what happened. It is something I have seen on several occasions to others, always with fatal results. Shortly after his plane had taken off, the motor in his plane quit. I know the terrain where the accident happened, having flown from the same field during the summer and fall of 1918. When the motor stopped there was no place for him to land without damaging his plane. This he was of course anxious to avoid, as he was the commanding officer of his squadron and been ordered to leave for America. He therefore tried to turn in order to get back to the field. When he did not have sufficient height to do so, the result was that he lost his flying speed, the plane went into a stall, slipped off on a wing, and struck the ground before he had a chance to regain control of the plane. If he had wanted to kill himself, he could have done so easily by diving into the ground instead of striving to extricate himself from his troubles as eyewitnesses described and the photos confirm.
>
> I understand that the reason given for this story is that Hobey had some difficulty with a girl. I know the girl in question (whose name I shall not mention) to whom he

had been engaged. When the engagement was broken off he was very much upset, but in my opinion, he had gotten over it before I left him.

Against all this you only have the word of whoever it was that started this miserable rumor. The word of anyone who would be mean and low enough to say such a thing about a courageous gentleman like Hobey Baker, even though he believed it to be true, is not, in my opinion, worthy of belief. [13]

Hobey's wealthy admirer Percy Pyne was a victim of the financial crash of 1929, eventually forfeiting his Long Island mansion for failure to pay back taxes. (Listerine)

Clockwise from top left: Percy Pyne, Mimi Scott, and Cole Porter all vied for Hobey's affections in 1918, the last year of his life. (Getty Images)

*Gifted pilots Eddie Rickenbacker (above) and Hobey Baker
(facing page) became good friends in France during World War I.
Rickenbacker was America's most decorated flying "Ace," while Hobey
spent much of the war frustrated on the sidelines. (Rickenbacker, Getty
Images; Baker, St. Paul's School)*

The remains of Hobey Baker's fatal last flight. His decision to return to the field with a dead engine remains a topic of heated debate a century later. (Princeton University)

The Grave of Capt. Hobart A.H. Baker '09

The American Aviator's cemetery in Toul, France. Baker was buried there for two years before his remains were returned to the United States. (St. Paul's School)

The "Rosetta Stone" of Hobey Baker mythology. The haunting poem on Baker's tombstone in suburban Philadelphia was labeled "anonymous" for nearly a century, until the mystery was finally solved by J. P. Archer. (St. Paul's School)

Alfred Thornton Baker and his son, Hobart Amory Hare Baker.
(St. Paul's School)

Parental Postscript

Alfred Thornton Baker

The last recorded letter from Hobey to his father contained within Princeton's Baker Collection is dated November 21, 1918. He reported to his father about his lunch that day in the village of Toul, where he purchased a Boche officer's spiked helmet, like the ones seen on the head of the Kaiser, along with an iron cross, a soldier's belt and buckle, and a canteen. The final paragraph reads as follows:

"I was officially ordered to a dance tonight where I danced with a girl who is going home. I said I would split my souvenirs with her if she would get my share to you in Princeton. She said she would, so they may show up some day." [1]

Because of the theft of Hobey's effects at the Orléans train station, nothing material from Hobey's life made it back from France, except for the souvenirs transported by Hobey's final dance partner. Baker's father, wheelchair-bound in Princeton in the last year of his life, found himself entertaining a young female visitor who just returned from France, a woman who had shared Hobey's last dance. After she exited, Bobby Baker remained holding the farewell keepsakes from Hobey in his lap—a spiked German officer's helmet and an iron cross, haunting souvenirs from the war that took his son's life.

According to his death certificate, Alfred Thornton Baker died from the condition *locomotor ataxia*, also known as *tabes dorsalis*. [2] He was 57 years old when he passed away. His symptoms were described frequently in letters; Davies referred to him as an "invalid" by age 50. [3] The definition of *tabes dorsalis,* and its cause, gives one pause. The U.S. National Library of Medicine identifies *tabes dorsalis* as "a complication of untreated syphilis." Symptoms include joint damage, loss of coordination, bladder control issues and problems with sexual function. [4] Mary and Bobby's "mutual dereliction" during their married years in Philadelphia may have earned Mary a scarlet letter of shame, but it dealt Hobey's father a slow and painful death sentence.

Mary Pemberton Van Shutts

Hobey's mom outlived her son and two husbands, but the last years of her life were marked by near poverty and cancer. She had exchanged several letters with the management of West Laurel Hill Cemetery, frequently deferring payments because of her reduced circumstances. When she passed away from cancer in 1948, her body was cremated, but there was no one left to settle her account at the Cemetery; her first son Thornton had long since moved to Lyme, Connecticut, and Percy was ailing out in California. Thus, Mary's inability to settle her account with West Laurel Hill Cemetery prevented her headstone from being placed next to her second husband and son, as originally intended. Her cremation is documented, but the whereabouts of her remains are unaccounted for. Once again, the dogged J.P. Archer devoted ample shoe-leather in his attempt to solve yet another ancient mystery.

Letters from Mary Van Shutts to her creditors at the cemetery reveal how tight her finances were in those final years. Real estate records show that she had sold Hobey's Southampton farmhouse in 1928, and struggled with her mortgage. In her later years, she was documented bouncing from home to home in the Philadelphia area, and when her husband Frederick died of a stroke in 1944, she used all her savings and her powers of persuasion to convince the West Laurel Hill Cemetery personnel to extend the family plot, and place Frederick's small headstone next to Hobey's. Nearly destitute four years later, Mary died of cancer on March 28, 1948. She was soon cremated, with the intention of joining her husband and son in lot number 12. But her finances were in arrears, and with no one to advocate on her behalf, her headstone never joined those of her family. Her remains are classified as "missing…location of ashes unknown." [5]

Archer, the amateur sleuth who became captivated by the unfinished business of Baker's life and legend, established a relationship with the employees at West Laurel Hill. They confided in him that it was not uncommon to put the remains of a loved one, like Mary, into its designated spot even with an outstanding bill. Then they described the process. [6] Archer, a man who learned first-hand how the Bala Cynwyd cemetery conducts its business, is convinced that Mary Pemberton's ashes were interred directly above Hobey's grave in West Laurel Plot 12. After being separated for 46 years, mother and child were finally united, in perpetuity.

Hobey Baker's Anonymous Epitaph

by Joseph Patrick Archer

I n the spring of 1991, a friend of mine clipped an article out of his new issue of *Sports Illustrated* and mailed it to me with spare but emphatic advice: "Read this now." It was Ron Fimrite's haunting essay, "A Flame That Burned Too Brightly," and it began in a remote corner of an old cemetery outside Philadelphia, at the little-known final resting place of Hobey Baker. There the author found a literal touchstone for his story: the modest granite slab bearing several lines of verse about a fleet and passionate mortal beckoned skyward by the gods — a poetic image that hinted, in Fimrite's words, at "the splendor of the man" interred below.

Splendor, indeed. As a schoolboy at St. Paul's in New Hampshire during the first decade of the 1900s, Hobart Amory Hare Baker —scion of a prominent Philadelphia family—impressed those lucky enough to see him at play as a compelling athletic prodigy. He dazzled at the recently imported game of ice hockey, but was a star, as well, in baseball, football, swimming and just about everything else he tried. Fast, powerful, quietly intense, joyfully competitive and supremely graceful, he seemed to possess a preternatural mastery of his own body in motion. (Upon request, he would casually walk up and down stairs—while standing on his hands.) Later, national newspapers chronicled Baker's spectacular performances on the Princeton University football and ice hockey teams as episodes in an unfolding legend. (They were right: he remains the only person ever inducted into the halls of fame for two different sports.) To boot, Baker's extraordinary physical gifts were paired with a humble, appealing and upright nature. He revered sportsmanship so deeply that the sight of underhanded play wounded him to the point of tears; and, after rare and bitter defeats, he would stride into the opposing locker room and warmly congratulate every man on the winning side. As though all that were not enough, he ventured from the ice-rinks and gridirons of collegiate games to the deadly skies over war-torn Europe and won the *Croix de Guerre* for heroism in aerial combat. But it was his fate — this golden boy of the nascent American Century—to die in his youth as the Great War ended, and then, with the slow-but-sure fading away of his generation, to slip from public memory.

Until we read the *Sports Illustrated* article, neither my friend nor I had ever heard of Hobey Baker, much less that he was buried only a few miles from where we had been students in the 1980s. But we were captivated by the tale of a glamorous scholar-athlete and World War I flyer and his fatal fall to the French countryside on the day before he was to return home. (Perhaps the fascination owed something to our affinity for the writings of F. Scott Fitzgerald, with which Baker's life shared not only thematic echoes but also a historical connection. Both men were at Princeton in the 1913-14 academic year, when Baker was a senior and Fitzgerald a freshman.) And so, when my friend and I met again near Philadelphia about six months after he sent me the article, we did what we probably subconsciously decided to do when we first read it: we headed to see Baker's grave for ourselves and to pay our respects to the once-renowned but now-forgotten tragic hero of playing fields and battlefields.

I still recall driving through the massive gates of West Laurel Hill Cemetery on a cold, damp late-October afternoon and sheepishly approaching a guardhouse to ask for help. After looking up the name and checking a map, the attendant gave us directions and we drove slowly on, past the marble mausoleums and other grand monuments to Philadelphia's departed nobility, and out to a field of much smaller headstones and flat markers at the far eastern edge of the vast cemetery. When we reached the approximate location, we parked the car and started wandering among the graves, reading unfamiliar names, until we came at last to the headstone we sought. The charismatic superstar, the brave pilot, the American Icarus, lay beneath our feet. Not another living soul was visible in any direction and only the intermittent patter of spitting rain on the leaf-covered ground disturbed the silence.

At the top of the headstone were Baker's full name, military rank and unit, the date and location of his death, and that awful phrase, "Aged 26 Years." Below, as Fimrite had recorded, eight lines of verse were etched in plain block capitals. We brushed aside a few wet leaves from the face of the stone and mumbled the words as we made them out in the thin light:

YOU WHO SEEMED WINGED, EVEN AS A LAD,
WITH THAT SWIFT LOOK OF THOSE WHO KNOW THE SKY,
IT WAS NO BLUNDERING FATE THAT STOOPED AND BADE
YOU BREAK YOUR WINGS, AND FALL TO EARTH AND DIE,
I THINK SOME DAY YOU MAY HAVE FLOWN TOO HIGH,
SO THAT IMMORTALS SAW YOU AND WERE GLAD,
WATCHING THE BEAUTY OF YOUR SPIRITS FLAME,
UNTIL THEY LOVED AND CALLED YOU AND YOU CAME.

We milled around the site for a while and imagined scenes of Baker's spellbinding athletic feats at St. Paul's and Princeton, of his daring prop-plane exploits in Europe, and of the long, lonely journey his still-young but lifeless body must have taken to this place. Before we walked away, we touched the top of the headstone, an instinctive gesture of reverence and affection for someone we never knew.

During the twenty-odd years that followed that day, I gradually forgot many of the particulars I must have known back then about Hobey Baker. But I never forgot the *feeling* of the Baker story. And, although I had not memorized the poem on his headstone and could not have recited even a single line of it, I always remembered that there *was* a poem — something about flying close to the angels — and that it seemed perfectly to capture, if not indeed to help create, the almost impossibly heroic, tragic, sad, romantic and mythical tale of Hobey Baker.

In early 2014, the Hobey Baker story popped back into my head. Actually, what came to mind was only what I vaguely recalled of the story, and I wanted to re-familiarize myself with the details. Fimrite's 1991 *Sports Illustrated* article was available online, and reading it again was a pleasure. Eventually, I also found and read John Davies' seminal 1966 biography, *The Legend of Hobey Baker*; Mark Goodman's 1985 biographical novel, *Hurrah for the Next Man Who Dies*; Emil Salvini's 2005 biography, *Hobey Baker, American Legend*; and Richard Stiles Greeley's 2014 commentary, *Tempting Fate*, on writings by Robert Stiles and Hobey Baker from the frontlines in 1918.

All of those books provided much information about Baker's character, life and world, but all of them left one question unanswered: *Who wrote that verse on the headstone?* Davies, Goodman, Salvini, Greeley and others, like Fimrite, quote the lines admiringly but treat them as anonymous and leave it at that. I couldn't help but wonder: Were they written *about* Hobey Baker, or just borrowed for his epitaph? Were they published or otherwise known before being engraved on that stone? On a couple of occasions, I googled certain phrases from the poem;

but the only hits I got were references back to Hobey Baker's headstone. I could find nothing that even asked, much less answered, who wrote it.

My curiosity led me to seek out original historical documents that might shed light on the epitaph. In that connection, one of the first places I visited was the Lower Merion Historical Society, which covers Bala Cynwyd, the Philadelphia suburb that is often identified as Baker's birthplace (and in which West Laurel Hill Cemetery is located). Upon arriving in the reading room, I whispered to a gentleman on the staff that I was researching a certain person who lived in the area around 1900, a prominent college athlete named Hobey Baker. From across the room, a voice immediately called out, *"Hobey Baker?! I caught somebody demolishing his house a few years ago and stopped it before they pulled down the last wall!"*

And thus I had the good fortune to meet Bob McCormick, a longtime Society volunteer, who personally collected many of the documents in its small file on Baker. He helped me with historical resources and shared with me his work, many years ago, establishing that Hobey was born not in Bala Cynwyd (as stated by Davies, Fimrite, Salvini and others), but in the Wissahickon neighborhood of Philadelphia proper. (The tidy, attractive, middle-class house still stands today, inhabited no doubt by a family utterly unaware of their distinguished predecessor.) And Bob identified for me the grand mansion on St. Asaph's Road in Bala Cynwyd to which the Bakers moved in 1900. (Due to Bob's intervention during the unauthorized demolition, the owner was required to rebuild so that the new façade matched the old one.)

When I first mentioned to Bob that I was interested in the headstone poem, he immediately remarked, "Oh, yeah, his mother wrote that," *Ah-ha, so that was the answer,* I thought. I asked Bob how he knew. He paused for a moment and then said he couldn't remember exactly, but that he felt fairly sure about it. Later, he explained that he might have simply *assumed* Hobey's mother was the author because she managed all the arrangements for Hobey's re-interment at West Laurel Hill. Even absent proof, I figured Bob's answer probably was right (I'd never heard any other attribution) and expected that I might find confirmation in historical records about Hobey's reburial.

When Hobey died in France in December 1918, his father, who was then living in Princeton, was most likely considered his next-of-kin, with ultimate authority over disposition of the body. And, indeed, documentation survives indicating that the personal effects Hobey left behind in France were gathered and prepared for delivery to his father. But Mr. Baker died in 1920. And, thus, by the time Hobey's body was returned to the U.S. the following year, Hobey's mother probably had legal control of it. If the Bakers had originally planned to re-inter Hobey at their own prominent site in Princeton's historic cemetery, those plans were upended by the transfer of authority to Hobey's mother. She was very likely estranged from the Baker clan since her acrimonious divorce when Hobey was 11 years old. And she ensured that Hobey would be buried in her own family plot at West Laurel Hill in Bala Cynwyd, personally directing the re-interment in July 1921 and the placement of the headstone in March 1922.

While reviewing files at the cemetery office one day, I found the original approval form for Hobey's headstone, which included a hand-drawn sketch of it. To my dismay, no inscription was shown; but the form did reveal the name of the company that prepared the stone. A few days' work enabled me to track down the successor company, which I phoned and visited in the hope that records for the headstone survived and might indicate the source of the poem. Unfortunately, the company's staff reported (after much pestering from me) that they no longer had any records from that time. My lead had reached a dead end; if anything was ever going to prove that Hobey's mother did or didn't write the poem, it would not be records relating to the re-burial.

From time to time, as I continued looking for historical documents that could be relevant, I'd wonder whether Hobey's mother, a woman of no known literary interests or accomplishments, *could* have written the epitaph. I found myself studying the composition carefully, as though it might reveal something about the author.

Simple, direct, conventional and sentimental, the poem nonetheless bore the marks of a serious, careful and practiced wordsmith. It scanned perfectly in iambic pentameter, with exactly ten syllables in each line, and had a disciplined rhyme scheme: A,B,A,B,B,A,C,C. (The scan pattern convinced me that "winged" was meant to be read as the two-syllable "wing-ed" and "blundering" as the elided "blund'ring".) Conceptually, as well, the poem appeared to show skilful design. Despite the curious appearance of a comma (rather than a period) after "die" in the fourth line, it essentially consisted of two parallel sentences, each of which captured a two-part thought. The first sentence described a mundane explanation for the subject's death (dumb luck/accident) and why the narrator rejects that explanation (the subject was too skilful to have suffered such an accident). The second sentence described a fanciful, uplifting alternative explanation (the gods' desire for the subject's company) and why the narrator finds it plausible (the gods saw the subject's beauty while he was aloft).

Did the poem's *content and quality* make Hobey's mother a more likely—or less likely—candidate for having written it? I went back and forth on that question. According to census records, she had only a fifth-grade education; but letters she penned in middle age show that she could write fluid, grammatically correct prose (and in quite a fancy cursive). The poem's opening focus on the subject as a child might betray a maternal perspective. And a few aspects of the composition could be signs of an amateur, rather than a professional, hand (*e.g.*, something out of kilter about the phrase, "the beauty of your spirits flame"). I couldn't rule her out, but I was not entirely convinced.

After a few months of local and online research, I turned my focus to Concord, New Hampshire. David Levesque, the archivist librarian at St. Paul's School, cheerfully spoke with me on several occasions about Hobey's time there and the school's collection of related memorabilia. As our discussions came to a close, I raised the subject of the epitaph. He replied that he had no idea who wrote it and had never met anyone who did.

The next stop was Princeton. Dan Linke at the university's Seeley G. Mudd Manuscript Library graciously met with me and provided an overview of the Hobey-related archives. Dan also put me in touch with Dick Greeley and Tim Rappleye. Dick had recently worked with the archives for his book, *Tempting Fate*. Tim, a hockey historian and writer, regaled me with his nearly-encyclopedic knowledge of the sport and its early players, and his special interest in Hobey Baker. To both I mentioned at some point my particular curiosity about the epitaph poem, but neither could recall seeing anything that cast light on its provenance.

Meanwhile I was burrowing deeply into the Princeton materials. The largest portion is the collection left by John Davies, which consists mainly of correspondence, notes and drafts from his writing of the 1966 biography (including more than a hundred letters Hobey wrote to his father and others from Europe during the war). A critical subset of the Davies collection is the material he obtained from Henry Baker, Hobey's nephew.

Hobey had only one sibling, a slightly older brother, named Thornton. As the boys finished prep school at St. Paul's, the family suffered financial setbacks that meant only one of them could attend Princeton (their father's and grand-father's *alma mater*)—a startling fracture in the life-arc on which both had been launched. Although the older of the two, Thornton stepped aside; and, while Hobey made his way to Old Nassau, Thornton went to work in a steel mill in Manayunk. Thornton eventually married Marie Griffiths Hall in 1914 (Hobey's senior year at Princeton) and they made their home for a time in Bala Cynwyd (only a mile or so from the St. Asaph's Road house of the boys' youth). Hobey briefly lived there with them before he departed for Europe and the war in July 1917.

Henry Baker was the fourth of Thornton and Marie's five

children, born in 1921, a couple of years after Hobey died. In about 1957, Henry set out to learn more about the famous uncle he had known primarily as a figure in scrapbook photographs. He solicited remembrances from Hobey's childhood friends, classmates, teammates, military buddies et al. and wove them into a long essay that he refined through many drafts in the hope of placing it in a magazine. Despite some interest and encouragement, that hope was never realized. Eventually, however, Henry turned over the essay, along with his drafts, research notes and correspondence, to Davies when Davies started his biography of Hobey in the mid-1960s. Henry's essay and source documents greatly impacted Davies' book and, by extension, almost everything written subsequently about Hobey.

On one autumn day, several months into my review of the Princeton archives, I was reading through some of the "Henry" files and came across several letters that Henry's mother, Marie, wrote to him about Hobey. (Evidently, Henry had cast his net near as well as far. And that was wise: his mother, Hobey's sister-in-law, was an especially important source for him, as she was Hobey's closest relative who was still alive at that time.) One of Marie's letters ended with this explicit reference to Hobey's epitaph:

Do you remember Amory's poem which was or is on his tombstone —

> *You who seemed wingèd*
> *Even when a lad—*
> *With that swift look*
> *Of those who know the sky—*
> *It was no idle Fate*
> *Who bade you break your wings*
> *And fall to earth & die—*
> *I think one day you must have*
> *Flown too high*
> *And So that Immortals saw you & were glad*

Watching the beauty of your spirit's flame
Until they called you
And you came!

*That poem I think was in sonnet form & should have 14
lines. My spacing of the lines is probably wrong. I'll try &
find the book it is in.*

That was the most extensive reference to the headstone poem
that I had ever seen in the historical documents and it raised
several fascinating questions. Why did Marie call it "Amory's
poem"? Was that the title of the piece? If so, perhaps it was not
written about Hobey, but rather borrowed for his epitaph. Or,
"Amory" could have been her nickname for Hobey (whose full
name was Hobart Amory Hare Baker), in which case, by "Amory's
poem," she simply meant "Hobey's poem." Most intriguing
for me was the possibility that "Amory's poem" referred to the
poem's author. If so, who was "Amory"; indeed, was "Amory" the
author's given name or surname? (I immediately doubted that
"Amory" referred to Hobey's mother because "Amory" was not
any part of her full name and Marie elsewhere calls her "May.")

Also notable were the differences between the poem as it
appeared in Marie's letter and on the headstone. Her line breaks
didn't match the headstone at all and, indeed, looked quite wrong;
"wingèd" had an accent grave (which, incidentally, showed that
she understood it as a two-syllable word, confirming my earlier
hunch); instead of "as a lad," she had "when a lad"; instead of "it
was no blundering fate that," she had "it was no idle Fate who";
instead of "stooped and bade you," she had simply "bade you";
instead of "watching the beauty of your spirits flame," she had
(to my mind, the more coherent) "watching the beauty of your
spirit's flame"; and instead of "Until they loved and called you,"
she had simply "Until they called you." The differences could be
explained simply as faulty recollection. (Marie was about 65 when
she wrote the letter.) But did they hint at something else: was she

recalling a version of the poem that was truly different in some particulars from the headstone version? And, if so, where was it? Marie mentioned that the poem was in a book in her possession. Did she mean a published book, or perhaps a family scrapbook in which someone copied the poem from the headstone?

One of the first things I did when I returned home after seeing Marie's letter was to google the phrase "Amory's poem." The results startled me: an array of references to F. Scott Fitzgerald's *This Side of Paradise*. That novel's protagonist is named "Amory Blaine" and some commentators suggest that Fitzgerald knew and liked the name "Amory" because of Hobey Baker, who was the superstar of Princeton during Fitzgerald's brief time there. (Hobey himself is most likely the model for a minor *Paradise* character, the football hero, Allenby.) I knew that Amory Blaine and other characters in the novel dabbled in poetry, but I did not recall anything specific. Could Hobey's epitaph possibly have originated in *This Side of Paradise*? (The timing worked: the novel was published in 1920, before the headstone was placed in 1922.) Although I was intrigued, I harbored doubts because I had long ago googled lines from the epitaph and had never seen any references to Fitzgerald.

I pulled my copy of *Paradise* off the shelf and quickly skimmed it. A dozen or more poems appear throughout the novel—everything from little couplets and ditties to much longer, more serious pieces, such as Amory's rejection of his social-climbing days and Father Darcy's musing about Amory's restlessness. And most importantly for my immediate purposes—*none of them was anything like the poem on Hobey's headstone*. Whatever Marie may have meant by "Amory's poem," she did not mean a poem by or about Amory Blaine in *This Side of Paradise*.

Next, I explored the possibility that "Amory" in Marie's letter was a reference to the poem's author. Since I knew "Amory" was one of Hobey's middle names, I started searching among his relatives for someone named Amory who might have been a writer. I found no one whose first name or surname was "Amory" but three who (like Hobey) had it as a middle name. All three were connected to Hobey through the marriage of one of his maternal aunts.

Hobey's mother, Mary Augusta Pemberton Baker, was a Philadelphia socialite with a knack for drawing the attention of newspaper columns with titles like "Just Gossip." (The Bakers' long-running marital troubles provided the Quaker city with years of scandalous amusement.) She was one of eight children, three boys and five girls. One of her older sisters, Rebecca, married a man named Hobart Amory Hare. Hare got his middle name from his mother, Mary Amory Howe. Hobart and Rebecca Hare had only one child, a daughter whom they named Mary Amory Hare. Those were my three "Amory"s.

Almost nothing emerged about Mary Amory Howe, who lived from 1837 to 1887. Of her son, Hobart Amory Hare, much more information came to light. He lived from 1862 to 1931 and became a distinguished physician, rising to the presidency of Thomas Jefferson Medical College. He married Rebecca Pemberton (Hobey's maternal aunt) in 1884 and was present at Hobey's birth in 1892. Presumably, Hobey's parents were very fond of Dr. Hare, as they named their new son "Hobart Amory Hare Baker." In researching Dr. Hare, I came across, for the first time, the sort of thing I was hoping to find: evidence of professional writing. Google searches on Dr. Hare produced hits to booksellers and reviews. As I tracked them down, I learned that he had authored influential medical textbooks, particularly on diagnosis. I found no sign of fiction or poetry; but here, at least, was an "Amory" who was a practiced author.

The third "Amory," Mary Amory Hare, was born to Hobart and Rebecca (Hobey's maternal aunt) in 1885. When at last, in November 2014, I got around to googling "Mary Amory Hare," I began to see references to old, out-of-print books whose author was identified by a variety of names: "Mary Amory Hare," "Amory Hare," "Amory Cook," "Amory Hutchinson," etc. Very quickly, it became apparent that at least some of the books were collections of poetry. Within less than an hour, I came upon a glittering nugget: an ad by a used-book dealer listing for sale a hardback volume of poetry by "Amory Hare" titled *Tossed Coins*. The publication date caught my eye: 1920 (*i.e.*, after Hobey's death in 1918 but before the placement of the headstone in 1922). I dug a bit deeper. The detailed sale listing included the table of contents, which showed that the poems were divided into three sections, "Joy O' Life," "In Sorrow" and "Quietude." The title of the second poem in the middle section was "To My Cousin." I bought the book online and waited.

It arrived a few days later, a small, slim volume with a tan canvas spine, stiff brown covers and soft, yellow-edged, hand-cut cotton paper. I opened it gently and leafed through to page 40, which bears only the words, "TO MY COUSIN." On the facing page:

> YOU who seemed winged, even when a lad,
> With that swift look of those who know the sky,
> It was no blundering Fate who stooped and bade
> You break your wings and fall to earth and die.
> I think one day you may have flown too high,
> So that Immortals saw you and were glad,
> Watching the beauty of your spirit's flame
> Until they loved and called you. . . . And you came.

Here was the book Marie must have meant; here was the version of the poem that she was recalling; and here was the solution to the mystery. Hobey Baker's epitaph was anonymous no longer. The author was his cousin, Mary Amory Hare, the daughter of his mother's sister Rebecca and Hobart Amory Hare, the man for whom Hobey was named.

Despite looking, I have discovered little that would show how close Mary and Hobey might have been. Until Hobey enrolled at St. Paul's in 1903 (when he was 11 and she was 18), Hobey and Mary both lived in the Philadelphia area and newspaper articles show that their families socialized together. Being seven years older, Mary would not have been a playmate of Hobey's; rather, she would have known him as a baby and a younger child and perhaps have been charmed by the daring, energetic child he must have been. Of their relationship as adults, I know nothing. (None of Hobey's surviving wartime letters mentions her.)

Although Mary Amory Hare's poetry now appears to be virtually unknown—I came across no commentary or criticism of her work and only one anthology (itself obscure) in which her work appeared—she seems to have written and published continuously through much of her life. Magazines such as *The Atlantic Monthly*, *Harper's* and *Scribner's* featured her poems for many years, starting in 1913, when she was 28. *Tossed Coins* was, as far as I can tell, her first published book; it was followed by *The Swept Hearth* (1922), *The Olympians* (1925), *Sonnets* (1927), *Deep Country* (1933) and *Between Wars* (1955). Much of her work was published by John Lane Company in New York, which was connected to the famous Bodley Head publishing house in London. In addition, several of Hare's works were adapted and produced on live television in the 1950s.

Of Mary Amory Hare's personal life, I managed to learn a few basic facts. She married an admiral, Arthur Cook, in 1908; they had two children, a daughter and a son, before divorcing. In 1927, she married a physician, James Hutchinson, who evidently had been a fine rower and football player at Harvard. In addition to writing, she was an accomplished painter and equestrian. She died at age 78 in California in 1964. In private conversations, her grand-daughter told me that Mary Amory Hare likely had little or no formal education beyond grammar school, but would have observed (and perhaps have participated in) the salon-type gatherings that her father hosted in their home for his medical colleagues and other erudite and sophisticated friends.

With the arrival of *Tossed Coins*, my investigation into the origins of Hobey Baker's epitaph had reached an end, except for one more, ironic discovery. I had noticed the following statement on the acknowledgements page of that book:

> THE author returns thanks for permission to use in this collection of her poems, those which have appeared in The Atlantic Monthly, Contemporary Verse, The Princeton Alumni Weekly and House and Garden.

The Princeton Alumni Weekly? I thought. Was it possible that "To My Cousin" appeared in that magazine even before it was published in Tossed Coins?

On my next trip to the Princeton archives, I asked if an index existed for the Weekly, which would allow one to find contributions by author or subject. The staff answered yes, and directed me to a large card catalogue in the lobby. I looked for Mary Amory Hare (and all the permutations of her name), but found no sign of her in the index. Nor was the poem among the many items indexed under Hobey Baker as subject. Still suspicious, I decided to do a manual search of the Weekly, just to be sure.

I knew that Hobey died on December 21, 1918, and that Tossed Coins was published in 1920. So, if the poem was first published in the magazine, then it would have to be in the 1919 or 1920 volume. I pulled the 1919 volume off the shelf and started skimming it, page by page. Page 570 of that volume (which is in the April 9, 1919, issue) contains a black-bordered text box in the lower left-hand corner. And in that box appears the following:

> To the memory of
> Hobart Amory Hare Baker
> Captain, 142nd Aero Squadron, A.E.F.
>
> YOU who seemed wingéd, even when a lad,
> With that swift look of those who know the sky,
> It was no blundering Fate who stooped and bade
> You break your wings and fall to earth and die.

I think one day you may have flown too high,
So that Immortals saw you and were glad,
Watching the beauty of your spirit's flame
Until they loved and called you . . . . .
And you came.
AMORY HARE

And thus I found myself staring at the very first appearance of the lines that were destined to become Hobey Baker's eulogy in granite.

While the authorship mystery has been solved, an attribution question remains. How did a twice-published work by a recognized professional poet come to be routinely presented as anonymous? That question leads back inexorably to Davies. Before writing the first Hobey Baker biography in 1966 (in which he showcased the lyrical epitaph), Davies had served more than a dozen years as Editor-in-Chief of the *Princeton Alumni Weekly* (where the poem first appeared, *signed by the author*). Furthermore, while writing the biography, Davies not only had in his possession Marie's letter to Henry, he also was in direct communication with Henry, who surely knew what Marie meant by "Amory's poem." Whether Davies simply failed to follow that clue, or did follow it and then chose to ignore what he learned, I do not know. (Ditto for subsequent biographers, who have had access to the Davies papers for more than 50 years.) In either event, it was Davies who apparently set those eight lines of verse on their curious journey to fame as Hobey Baker's "anonymous" epitaph — and set me on my unexpected adventure as an amateur literary detective.

[Note: *The three versions of the poem—the headstone version, the* Tossed Coins *version and the* Princeton Alumni Weekly *version*

—are reproduced exactly above. The 1919 Princeton Alumni Weekly version (i.e., the original) was published with only a few slight changes in the 1920 Tossed Coins collection. But the 1922 headstone version of the poem shows more substantial differences (e.g., 'when a lad' became 'as a lad'; 'spirit's' became 'spirits'; the period at the end of the fourth line became a comma), which are most likely corruptions owing to Hobey's mother's imperfect recollection or the stone carver's transcription errors.]

Acknowledgements

It was 6:00 p.m. on a December eve in Princeton back in 2013, and it felt like midnight. I had snaked my way through a long ally to the ancient Alchemist and Barrister pub; a stranger had sought me out to exchange information about a man who had been dead for nearly a century. It felt like I'd been inserted into a scene penned by Sir Arthur Conan Doyle.

A slight man, well-spoken and well-dressed, came precisely at the appointed hour and introduced himself as J.P. We took a table towards the rear, away from the holiday din. He had come to pick my brain about Hobey Baker, having heard of me from a fellow "Hobeyologist" whom I had guided through the Princeton archives. I soon realized that in terms of workable intelligence on the story of Hobey Baker, J.P. Archer was in a class by himself.

He was a powerful intellect, a former Rhodes scholar who shared editing duties at the Harvard Law Review with Barack Obama. He began firing questions at me.

Why wasn't Hobey buried in the Baker family plot in Princeton? Why was he interred in Bala Cynwyd when the Baker clan had pulled out of Philadelphia nearly a decade prior to Hobey's death? Where was Hobey's mother? What did I know about the anonymous verse on Hobey's gravestone? Didn't I have any clues?

I had entered this pub as the Hobey Baker answer man; I left in a cloud of confusion. Not only did I have no answers for J.P. regarding Hobey's Philadelphia chapter, but I wasn't sure where to begin. After an hour, the gentleman graciously picked up the bill for the soup and sandwich; I collected his contact information. J.P. Archer would prove to be a force in my efforts to unravel the mystery and history of Hobey Baker. He shared everything: his meticulous notes, photos of crucial letters, and his time on the phone in long, meandering calls. Archer's fascinating account of how he untangled the mystery of Hobey's headstone poem follows as this book's Afterword.

One of his great sources, Bob McCormick of the Lower Merion Historical Society, also proved eager to help my cause. Bob clued me in to the benefits of Hobey's original Philadelphia home when he sent me a 90-year old wintertime image of Wissahickon Creek, a frozen skating mecca packed with Philadelphia's finest on two blades.

The night of the initial meeting with Archer, I was accompanied by my son, Ted Rappleye, Princeton class of 2016. He proved to be a loyal ally and frequent companion in my *Hobey-quests* during his four years at Ol' Nassau. His contributions were many: he procured the book's cover photo from the school archives, unearthed a crucial six-page letter detailing Hobey's life in college, and stood by my side as we journeyed several stories under Jadwin Gymnasium in search of Hobey's missing portrait. It is a combination of a father's love and an author's gratitude that color my thanks to Ted.

My wife Amy is a loving wordsmith and a fabulous editor. She insisted on reading my chapters herself, on paper, and not let me regale her with my enthusiastic reads. She steered me away from tired cliché's and ingrained sports code to explain what, exactly, was happening on the ice and the gridiron.

Having an older brother who is an elite author gave me considerable comfort; every time I encountered a speedbump in either my writing or the publishing process, I simply picked up the phone and called Charles Rappleye in Los Angeles. He was always up early, working on his own projects when I called. I am profoundly grateful for his frequent counsel.

I spent considerable time in Princeton conducting research, frequently needing a place to spend the night. My oldest hockey comrade Joe McCarthy is a resident of Princeton, and along with his loving wife Livia, they opened up their guest room and their kitchen to me unconditionally, with or without notice. I would be in debtor's prison today if I had to fork out for hotel accommodations each night that I stayed with the McCarthy family.

New Jersey author and historian W. Barry Thomson was an absolute bulldog while conducting his enthusiastic research on Hobey's admirer Percy Pyne. The Pyne family has tentacles throughout wealthy Somerset County, New Jersey, and Thomson scoured them all in search for answers to the mysterious exit of Percy Rivington Pyne 2nd from New Jersey. Thomson was exceedingly patient when he helped me draw out the extensive Pyne family tree, one that contained three different relatives named Percy Pyne. Thomson tapped into his vast knowledge of New Jersey architecture to produce a video clip of Woodrow Wilson's stylish Tudor on Election Day 1912.

Pittsburgh hockey historian James Kubus was kind enough to speak to me by phone, a call in which he provided a scintillating re-enactment of his discovery of Hobey's final hockey game. That day began with him dutifully perusing one of the dozens of old scrapbooks given to him by one of Pittsburgh's elderly fans. He recalled how he found a 90-year-old ad promoting Baker's arrival in Pittsburgh, and the journey commenced. His website *PittsburghHockey.Net* is a treasure trove for hockey history buffs.

To the selfless librarians at the Seeley G. Mudd Manuscript Library at Princeton, a tip of the cap for all the patience they showed during each of my visits over the past two decades. Even when I lost the locker keys, they never showed any semblance of annoyance. Archivist David Levesque of St. Paul's School was always the consummate professional, consistently delivering more than what I asked. He was a vital asset to this project.

My parents, the Cromptons of Cambridge, once again turned over their living room to me whenever I rolled through town. My mother and I had a memorable afternoon debating the cause of Hobey's death. Initially she thought suicide, but that was before she was presented with the full extent of Hobey's letters pertaining to the subject.

Hockey historian Stephen Hardy spent an afternoon discussing Hobey with me in his New Hampshire home. We screened the documentary *Golden* while munching on his wife's freshly baked cookies. Not only did Steve share his considerable knowledge of Baker, but he forwarded several book chapters and magazine articles pertaining to Hobey and the origins of American hockey. The producer/writer of *Golden*, Paul Lally, was also generous with his time and opinions on Hobey. He was kind enough to guide me through the tripwires that accompany the procurement of century-old still photos. Former Yale Hockey captain Bruce Smith, one of the greatest Hobeyologists of them all, never failed to return a call when it came to discussing America's hockey deity.

The savvy publishing team of Mission Point Press up in Traverse City believed in Hobey from the get go. Editorial Director Anne Stanton frequently shared her conviction that regardless the time passed since Baker's death, he still was a splendid topic. Her brilliant graphic artist Heather Shaw helped bring America's hockey heartthrob back to life as soon as she was brought on board.

And finally, "Hockey Maven" Stan Fischler deserves special thanks for allowing me into his literary inner sanctum on Manhattan's upper west side. I had the honor of spending a night on his couch, surrounded by decades' worth of hockey books, photos, and mementos. The following morning I enjoyed a memorable stroll down Broadway, talking pucks with America's premier hockey historian.

If not for the selfless contributions of the aforementioned, this project could never have been completed.

NOTES ON SOURCES

Key Abbreviations:

Mudd = Seeley G. Mudd Manuscript Library, Princeton, NJ

Davies = *The Legend of Hobey Baker,* by John Davies. Little, Brown and Company 1966

Salvini = *Hobey Baker, American Legend,* by Emil R. Salvini. Hobey Baker Memorial Foundation 2005

Golden = "Golden, the Hobey Baker Story," Documentary Video, New Hampshire Public TV 2004

NYT = *New York Times*

PAW = *Princeton Alumni Weekly*

CHAPTER ONE: *Scandal!*

1. "...born into Philadelphia society..." McCormick, Robert. January 2018 correspondence and interview. Lower Merion Historical Society (LMHS), Bala Cynwyd, Penn. Note: McCormick and his peers at LMHS corrected the long-mistaken address of Hobey Baker's first home, Philadelphia, *not* Bala Cynwyd.
2. "...handsome woman with classic Grecian features ..." Conover, J.P., 1960 letter to John Davies; Mudd, Box 1 folder 2.
3. "...mutual dereliction..." Davies, page 5.
4. "...Quaker City Gossips..." Salvini, p. 6.
5. "We can't do much about this boy..." Tolan, Edward, October 5, 1959 letter to Davies; Mudd, Box 1, folder 2.
6. "...called a mental case..." Roberts, Elizabeth, 1960 letter to Davies; Mudd Box 4
7. "...committed to an asylum..." Packard, Parker, Interview, Golden.
8. "...intends to sail for Europe..." *Philadelphia Enquirer,* July 2, 1905

CHAPTER TWO: *Seven Years in the Cradle*

1. "Two sturdy little boys..." Conover, J.P., 1960 letter to John Davies; Mudd, Box 1, folder 2.
2. We flooded the field just below the dam..." Conover, Reverend James, 1915 letter. Ohrstrom Library, St. Paul's School, Concord, N.H.

3. "…one of the things that really hurt him…" Smith, Bruce, November 2017 Interview.
4. "…special little ponds that were well protected…." Bostwick, Pete, Jr., interview, Golden
5. "He could go out at night in the dark…" Baker, Hobart II, interview, Golden
6. "I haven't read about anybody as driven…" Smith interview *Ibid.*
7. "They would hide their skates…" Schley, John, January 2018 correspondence.
8. "Baker shined…" St. Paul's School notes from Mudd, Box 2.
9. "I had to go out and warn him…" *New York Tribune,* Jan 27, 1918
10. "He simply couldn't make his skates behave…" *New York Tribune, Ibid*
11. "Pandemonium," Davies, page 3.
12. "148 pounds" SPS Records, Mudd, Box 2
13. Hobey measurements, SPS, *Ibid.*
14. "O For the Wings of a Dove," Davies, p. 8
15. Hobey member of SPS Camera Club, SPS Records, Mudd Box 2
16. "He was very beautifully built…" Baker, Hobart II, interview, Golden
17. "Men liked Hobey…" Herring, Donald, Feb. 5, 1959 letter to Andrew Turnbull, Mudd, Box 1, folder 2
18. "She became fond of them both…" Conover, J.P., 1960 letter to John Davies, Mudd Box 1, folder 2
19. Hobey's new hockey skates. Conover, Reverend James, 1960 letter to John Davies, Mudd, Box 4
20. "Swam before every meal in the nude," Conover, J.P., 1960 letter to John Davies, Mudd, Box 1, folder 2.
21. "Hobey had perfect control of himself…" Davies p. 9
22, "…he also had intense dedication…" Hardy, Stephen, interview, Golden
23. Giant swings on high bar; Davies p. 14
24. "Permanent adolescence." Davies p. 6
25. "Let Hobey be the star…" Baker, Hobey II, interview, Golden

CHAPTER THREE: *Hockey Purgatory*

1. "…45 players died playing football…" *Washington Post* 5/29/2014
2. Rules changed to save the sport, *Washington Post, Ibid.*

3. "Every five-yard stripe..." Davies p. 23

4. "...a degree of artistry..." Davis, Jerry, interview, Golden

5. "He could have played five sports..." Herring, Donald, Feb. 5 letter to Andrew Turnbull, Mudd Box 1, folder 2

6. Blackfoot Indian, Herring, *Ibid.*

7. "A light guy like me..." Davies p. 28.

8. "Sam White decides me..." Salvini p. 17

9. "Why he wasn't killed..." Davies p. 31

10. "...could not have been spared..." Davies p. 31

11. "...get in some skating..." Davies p. 25

12. "If father is man enough..." Edwards, William Hanford, *Football Days, Memories of the Game and Men Behind the Ball*, Moffat, Yard and Company, 1916, p. 262

CHAPTER FOUR: Here He Comes

1. "First American Superstar" Fischler, Stan, November 2017 interview.

2. "Long lines of limousine..." Davies, preface page *XX*

3. Williams hockey team as 'formidable." Salvini p. 52

4. "This was no enemy..." Salvini p. 57

5. Cleary describing getting fans out of their seats. Cleary, William, interview, Golden

6. Sports highs and recreational drugs, *Chemical Engineering News* October 5, 2015 "Exploring the Molecular Basis of a Runner's High"

7. "...looking at him wears me out..." Davies p. 23

8. Newspaper headline montage, Davies p. 50

9. Montreal fans "Hobey, Hobey, Hobey," Salvini p. 56

10. "It's hard to be a great athlete," Price, Jerry, interview, Golden.

11. Dashing atop the dasher, Davies p. 48

12. "More graceful than any dancer..." Cushing, Holbrook, 1960 letter to John Davies, Mudd Box 1, folder 2

13. "That penalty could cost them the game!" Davies p. 51

14. "...zig-zag dashes..." *NYT* Jan 19, 1913

15. "...his face wet with tears..." Davies p. 52

16. "A good deal of betting..." Davies p. 44

17. "When Baker started up the ice..." Saltonstall, Senator Leverett, March 23, 1962 letter to George Frazier, Mudd Box 2

18. "Winsor taught us to keep our lanes..." Saltonstall, Ibid.

19. "…but the game was saved…" Saltonstall, Ibid.
20. "Wasn't even breathing hard." Davies p. 44
21. "Break the tie…" Salstonstall letter
22. Three wins in 26 hours. Salvini p. 60
23. "Without a doubt the greatest…" *NYT* Feb. 5, 1983, quoting the 50 year old *Boston Journal* story on Hobey..
24. "Scotch and Soda…" Bauhan, Rolf, April 27, 1962 letter to George Frazier, Mudd, Box 4.

CHAPTER FIVE: Biggest Man on Campus

1. "He was absolutely fearless." Davies, p. 20.
2. Wilson's third visit to FB practice. Davies 28.
3. "Good night pursuers…" *Boston Herald* October 13, 1912.
4. Louden newspaper clip. Davies, p. 74.
5. "I don't think it interested him…" Kuhn, Wendel, 1960 letter to John Davies, Mudd, Box 4.
6. "…led out of the back of the Arena…" Davies, p. 62.
7. "…he would be just as high…" Emmons, Thornton, December 12, 1959 letter to John Davies, Mudd, Box 1, folder 2.
8. "…the night he streaked…" Azoy, Anastozio, 1960 letter to John Davies, Mudd.
9. "…high above Central Park South…" Davies p. 61.
10. "…that wonderful, beautiful body." Beyer, Henry, 1960 letter to John Davies, Mudd, Box 1, folder 2.
11. "None of which went to his head." Shackleford, W.T., 1960 letter from to Davies, Mudd, Box 1, folder 2.
12. "He hated publicity…" Bauhan, Rolf, April 27, 1962 letter to George Frazier, Mudd, Box 4.
13. "The type of male animal…" Herring, Donald, Feb. 5, 1959 letter to Andrew Turnbull, Mudd Box 1, folder 2.
14. "Hobey despised pomposity." Herring *Ibid.*
15. "Tears in Hobey's eyes…" Underhill, 1960 letter to John Davies, Mudd, Box 1, folder 2.
16. "But along came Hobey with a smile…" Davies, p. 60
17. "I was afraid you weren't going to stop me…" Fimrite, Ron, *Sports Illustrated,* March 18, 1991, "A Flame that Burned Too Brightly."
18. "…who stood within ten feet of me." Mizener, Arthur, *Far Side of Paradise,* Houghton Mifflin, 1951, Chapter 4.

19. "…the football captain, slim and defiant…" Fitzgerald, F. Scott, *This Side of Paradise,* Cambridge University Press, 1995, p. 46.

20. "…detached and breathlessly aristocratic." Fitzgerald, *Ibid,* page 51.

21. "…attended class, nonchalant and calm." Tippetts, William, 1960 letter to Davies, Mudd Box 1, folder 2.

22. "The Princeton captain alone could save Princeton." Salvini, p. 49.

23. "50,000 words in preparation." Davies, p. 57.

24. "Only a fair student." McColl, J. Robertson, 1960 letter to Davies, Mudd Box 1, folder 2.

25. "…there was the great Hobey Baker!" Davies, p. 73.

26. "His untimely passing…" Beyer, Henry, 1960 letter to Davies, Mudd Box 1, folder 2.

27. "…an unconscionable and ill-mannered snob." Blair, Paxton, 1960 letter to John Davies, Mudd Box 1, folder 2.

28. "Too aloof to slap rumps…" Davies p. 39.

29. "Hobey could wedge a pencil…" Beyer letter, *Ibid.*

30. List of Hobey's favorite tunes. Davies, p. 69.

31. "You would oblige me by saying nothing at all." Davies, p.73.

HOBEYQUEST: Baker's Stand-in

1. The week prior to Princeton's 2018 graduation, I paid a second visit to the campus library, and received a hot lead in my search for the Peter Cook Hobey Portrait. I was given the name *Lisa Arcomano,* Princeton's manager of campus collections. I emailed her straight away, attaching an image of the Cook painting. She responded within hours. Arcomano was familiar with the work, reporting that it had been removed from Dillon Gym in 2001 and placed in Museum storage, possibly because of renovation being done in its vicinity. Arcomano concluded her note with the following statement: "I'll be happy to check with the Athletics department to see if they can find an appropriate home for the work."

CHAPTER SIX: The Sprint to the Hall of Fame

1. "America's best-known athlete." Bauhan, Rolf, April 27, 1962 letter to George Frazier, Mudd, Box 4.

2. "…immediately tried to enlist." Davies, 91.

3. "Think of all the things…" Davies p. 78.

4. "One man's brilliant speed…" Davies, p. 85.
5. "Slashed and kicked in the knee…" Davies p. 85.
6. "…knocked him out." Davies p. 82.
7. "Forget it, it's part of the game." Davies, p. 82.
8. "Those fellows want to rough me up." Davies, p. 82.
9. "Masochistic orgies…" Rappleye, W.C. Jr. 2012 interview. Note: Willard Rappleye worked for Time, Inc. from 1950 to 1960, writing occasionally for *Sports Illustrated*, primarily for *Time Magazine*.
10. "Bowels of the earth…" Kuhn, Wendel, 1960 letter to John Davies, Mudd, Box 4.
11. "…the temperature of his bath." Davies, p. 65.
12. "…we're as good or better than them." Fischler, Stan, November 2017 interview.
13. Hobey was listed as a "centre." *Montreal La Presse*, December 12, 1915.
14. "…cooked our goose so artistically…" Davies, p. 88.
15. "…could be a star…" Davies p. 87.
16. "Lucky to get out alive." Davies p. 89.
17. "I won't play…" Dickey, Charles, 1960 letter to John Davies, Mudd Box 1, folder 2.
18. "…diamond gold medal…" Trimble, Rufus, 1960 letter to John Davies, Mudd Box 1, folder 2.
19. "Babe Ruth of hockey…" Fischler, *Ibid*.
20. "…to insure immortality." Frazier, George, *Boston Herald*, essay, December 1962. Note: George Frazier was Boston's premier essayist, and his 1962 ode to Hobey was one of his finest, most memorable works. If not for the Davies biography published four years later, it would be the Frazier essay that would be the piece that linked Hobey Baker to readers in the latter part of the 20th century.

CHAPTER SEVEN: King of Hockey II

1. "That puck really flew on that black ice…" Cleary, Bill, interview, October 2017.
2. "…began to use Cleary as a rover." *St. Paul's Record* 1951.

CHAPTER EIGHT: Drums of War

1. "Savors of anticlimax…" Fitzgerald, F. Scott. *The Great Gatsby*, Charles Scribner and Sons, Chapter 1.

2. "...prejudiced leach on society." Daniel, Anne Margaret, November 2017 interview.
3. "No matter how long I live..." Beck, James, December 12, 1959 letter, to Henry Baker, Mudd, Box 1, folder 2.
4. "...tragic death was not far off." Beck, *Ibid.*
5. "...America's first aerial knights." *NYT* April 24, 1933.
6. "Aviation appealed to me..." Salvini p. 84.
7. "Hobey had been ruled ineligible..." *NYT* November 18, 1916.
8. "They dipped, spiraled, and looped-the-loop." *NYT* November 19, 1916.
9. "...throngs in orange and black." *NYT Ibid.*
10. "...death to our young men." National Archives, *Prologue Magazine,* Spring 2017, Vol. 49, No. 1
11. "It just came naturally to me..." *Pittsburgh Press,* May 22, 1917

CHAPTER NINE: Fraternal Encore

1. "He was very much a hero..." Baker, Hobey II interview, Golden.
2. "...a new front tooth for Easter." Baker, Marie, 1960 letter to Henry Baker, Mudd Box 1, folder 2.
3. "The story first appeared..." *Pittsburgh Tribune Review,* December 27, 2010
4. "Hobey Baker played a final game..." Allen, Kevin, *Star Spangled Hockey,* Triumph Books 2011, chapter 1.
5. Kubus' impeccable sourcing. *PittsburghHockey.net*
6. "T. Baker as Hobey's brother Tommy." *Pittsburgh Dispatch,* March 25, 1917.
7. Poster: "Hobey Baker, America's Greatest Hockey Star." *PittsburghHockey.Net*
8. "Puck drop at 8:15 p.m." *Pittsburgh Gazette* March 25, 1917.
9. "Machine Hall refrigeration plant..." *PittsburghHockey.Net*
10. "Here he comes!" *Pittsburgh Press* March 25, 1917.
11. "12 shots off of Ford's stick..." *Pittsburgh Dispatch* March 25, 1917.
12. "...pushing one past Chislett." *Pittsburgh Dispatch, Ibid.*
13. "...made the difference." *Pittsburgh Dispatch, Ibid.*

CHAPTER TEN: Who was Percy Pyne

1. "...fair-haired younger men." Kuhn, Wendel, 1960 letter to John Davies, Mudd, Box 4.

2. "I can't imagine Hobe being happy…" Kuhn *Ibid*.
3. "Hobey was the cat's meow." Packer, Parker, interview, Golden.
4. "Hobey had stayed at Percy's…" Bauhan, Rolf, April 27, 1962 letter to George Frazier, Mudd, Box 4.
5. "Poster child for the idle rich…" Thomson, W. Barry, October 2017 interview.
6. "Sort of continuous vaudeville…" *NYT,* October 17, 1950.
7. "…not done in conservative society." Thomson interview, *Ibid*.
8. "…failure to pay his back taxes." *NYT* October 17, 1950.
9. "…she chose to say nothing." Thomson, W. Barry, 2009 correspondence.
10. "I resent this sort of gossip…" Kuhn letter, *Ibid*.

CHAPTER ELEVEN: The Great War, Part I "Hurry Up an Wait"

1. "God knows I have not deserved…" Baker, Hobey, July 23, 1917 letter to Percy Pyne, Mudd, Box 1, folder 1.
2. "…long and frustrating experience…" Woolley, Charles, interview, Golden.
3. "Lord knows how glad I would be…" Baker, Hobey, October 4, 1917 letter to Percy Pyne, Mudd, Box 1, folder 1.
4. "You certainly have been good to mother." Hobey letter, *Ibid*.
5. "Why you should be so good to me…" Hobey letter, *Ibid*.
6. "A vivid dream/You look so clean and nice/I wish to heaven you would come over…" Baker, Hobey, October 10, 13, 17, 1917 letters to Percy Pyne, Mudd, Box 1.
7. "They shoot in every known way…" Baker, Hobey, October 4, 1917 letter to Percy Pyne, Mudd, Box 1, folder 1.
8. "…gave him up for lost." Biddle, Charles, *Princeton Alumni Weekly,* January 15, 1919.
9. "…surest way to die." Biddle, *Ibid*.
10. "I was about to be killed…" Baker, Hobey, October 25, 1917 letter to Percy Pyne.
11. "I'm a ghost/If I go west/Couldn't be a nicer way to die…" Baker, Hobey, letter compilation, Mudd.
12. "Handle your machine… just as you do when rushing the ball." Baker, Hobey, March 12, 1918 letter to father, Mudd Box 1, folder 1.

13. "I'll get a Boche, or he will get me..." Baker, Hobey, February 4, 1918 letter to father, Mudd Box 2, folder 1.

14. "Making violent love..." Baker, Hobey, November 12, 1917 letter to Percy Pyne, Mudd Box 1, folder 1.

15. "...bump on my head, which knocked me silly." Baker, Hobey, January 13, 1918 letter to father, Mudd Box 1, folder 1.

16. "I wish you could see how bold I am." Baker, Hobey, January 19, 1918 letter to Percy Pyne, Mudd Box 1, folder 1.

17. Life Insurance "...paid directly to the boys' mother Mary." Salvini, page 103.

18. "Cheap newspaper name." Baker, Hobey, January 13, 1918 letter to father, Mudd Box 1, folder 1.

19. "...killed by a taxi before I get to the front." Baker, Hobey, February 8, 1918 letter to Percy Pyne, Mudd, Box 1, folder 1.

20. *Princeton Alumni Weekly* February 6, 1918.

21. "I almost fainted..." Baker, Hobey, April 3, 1918 letter to father, Mudd Box 1, folder 1.

22. "I met a very attractive girl..." Baker, Hobey, February 4, 1918, letter to father, Mudd Box 1, folder 1.

23. "Absolutely delightful..." Baker, Hobey, February 8, 1918 letter to Percy Pyne, Mudd, Box 1, folder 1.

24. Victor Chapman "Addicted to danger..." St. Paul's School Archives, *The Roll of Honor: St. Paul's School in the Great War*

25. "...officers in the road scattered like chickens." Baker, Hobey, March 8, 1918 to father, Mudd, Box 1, folder 1.

26. "Brother airmen say they can recognize Baker anywhere..." *NYT* January 3, 1918

27. "...he was an outstanding player, he was part of a team." Cleary, Bill, interview, Golden.

28. "...there couldn't be a nicer way to die." Baker, Hobey, April 12, 1918, letter to father, Mudd, Box 1, folder 2.

29. "I am courting danger daily..." Baker, Hobey, April 21, 1918, Hobey letter to Percy Pyne, Mudd, Box 1, folder 2.

30. "She would certainly do for a wife..." Baker, Hobey, April 3, 1918 letter to father, Mudd, Box 1, folder 1.

1. "This certainly is a big league game…" Baker, Hobey, April 23, 1918 letter to father, Mudd Box 1, folder 2.
2. Biddle's plane turned over. Baker, Hobey May 15, 1918 letter to father, Mudd, Box 1, folder 2.
3. Biddle sprinting 50 yards on a bum leg. Baker, Hobey, May 16, 1918 letter to father, Mudd, Box 1, folder 2.
4. "I miss Charley Biddle…" Baker, Hobey, May 21, 1918 letter to father, Mudd, Box 1, folder 2.
5. Description of the massive dogfight. Baker, Hobey, May 21, 1918 letter to father, Mudd, Box 1, folder 2.
6. "I wish she did not have so much money…" Baker, Hobey, May 23, 1918 letter to father, Mudd, Box 1, folder 2.
7. "What will I marry her on?" Baker, Hobey, April 21, 1918 letter to Percy, Mudd, Box 1, folder 1.
8. "I have certainly done nothing as yet to be very proud of…" Baker, Hobey, June 23, 1918 letter to Percy, Mudd, Box 1, folder 2.
9. "The most wonderful thing that has happened to me…" July 9, 1918 letter to Percy. Mudd, box 1, folder 2.
10. "Cold, no charm, no sweetness." Biddle, Charles, June 24, 1966 letter to John Davies, Mudd, box 4.
11. "Gridiron Star Baker is Now an American Ace." Davies, page 98.
12. Letter montage of bad luck. Baker, Hobey, July 22-August 6, 1918 letters to father, Mudd, Box 1, folder 2.
13. "Wonderful, absolutely ideal…" Baker, Hobey August 18, 1918 letter to father, Mudd, Box 1, folder 2.
14. "Run it like Thornton would…" Baker, Hobey, August 8, 1918 letter to father, Mudd, Box 1, folder 2.
15. "…a large surplus of recreational drugs." Cole Porter Wikipedia site; reference: *The Cole Porter Resource site,* J. Christopher Bell.
16. "We sang, he played…" Baker, Hobey, August 15, 1918 letter to father, Mudd, Box 1, folder 2.
17. "…wearing a bogus custom-made uniform in order to impress his guests." Salvini, page 98.
18. "Always the same, delay and mistake." Baker, Hobey, August 15, 1918 letter to father, Mudd, Box 1, folder 2.
19. "Went to a Cole Porter party…" Baker, Hobey, August 20, 1918 letter to father, Mudd, Box 1, folder 2.

20. "...nothing to do except make the best of it here." Baker, Hobey, September 2, 1918 letter to father, Mudd, Box 1, folder 2.
21. Hobey making evening phone calls to Biddle. Baker, Hobey, September 17, 1918 letter to father, Mudd, Box 1, folder 2.
22. "...he has struck rum luck from the start." Biddle, Charles, *The Way of the Eagle,* Read Books, Ltd, 2013. Originally published 1919.
23. "I know how he frets..." Biddle *Ibid.*
24. Hobey searching for Mimi in Paris. Baker, Hobey, September 3, 1918 letter to father, Mudd Box 1, folder 2.
25. "I gave her up." Hobey letter, *Ibid.*
26. A close acquaintance of Percy's. Hobey, *Ibid.*
27. "Come see me." *Ibid.*
28. "It's all fixed and we are engaged." Hobey, *Ibid.*
29. "Popular Leader of Newport Set..." Davies, page 99.
30. "If I could only see Mimi..." Baker, Hobey, September 25, 1918 letter to Percy Pyne, Mudd, Box 1, folder 2.
31. "She sort of worries me now..." Baker, Hobey, October 12, 1918 letter to father, Mudd, Box 1, folder 2.
32. "I sure am good when it comes to girls." Baker, Hobey, October 13-20, 1918 letter to father, Mudd, Box 1, folder 2.
33. "It may be rah-rah..." Baker, Hobey, October 23, 1918 letter to Wendel Kuhn, Mudd Box 4.
34. "Boy, that fellow..." Woolley, Charles, interview, Golden. Note: Woolley is quoting anonymous pilot's journal.
35. "It's damn unpleasant." Baker, Hobey, October 29, 1918 letter to father, Mudd, Box 1, folder 2.
36. "Leg blown off...burst out crying." Baker, Hobey, October 28, 1918 letter to father, Mudd, Box 1, folder 2.
37. "I would have given up command..." Baker, Hobey, October 29, 1918 letter to father, Mudd, Box 1, folder 2.
38. "I would recognize him on the street..." Baker, Hobey, October 30, 1918 letter to father, Mudd, Box 1, folder 2.
39. "He fell two and a half miles..." Baker, Hobey, November 16, 1918 Hobey letter to Percy Pyne, Mudd, Box 1, folder 2.
40. "Height of efficiency..." Baker, Hobey, November 11, 1918 letter to father, Mudd, Box 1, folder 2.
41. "I put her down in a field." Baker, Hobey, November 11, 1918 letter to father, Mudd, Box 1, folder 2.

CHAPTER THIRTEEN: *The Crash of 1918*

1. "I felt like a fool…" Baker, Hobey, November 21, 1918 letter to father, Mudd Box 1, folder 2.

2. "To get back is Oh!…" Baker, Hobey, November 8, 1918 letter to father, Mudd Box 1, folder 2.

3. Locks of his nephew's hair. Baker, Hobey, referenced in September 29, 1918 letter to father, Mudd Box 1, folder 2.

4. Father confined to a wheel chair. Bauhan, Rolf, April 27, 1962 letter to George Frazier, Mudd Box 4.

5. Bauhan said Baker was eager to get home to celebrate. Bauhan *Ibid.*

6. "…hated the idea of being killed right at the finish." Baker, Hobey, November 16, 1918 letter to Percy Pyne, Mudd, Box 1, letter 4.

7. "…your influential friends can do something for me." Hobey letter to Pyne, *Ibid.*

8. "…damned glad to see him." Hobey letter to Pyne, *Ibid.*

9. "…to ask for a change in orders." Herring, Donald, February 5, 1959 letter to Davies, Mudd, Box 4.

10. "Swishing orders in faces…" Davies, page 105.

11. "…one last flight in the old Spad." Davies, *Ibid.*

12. "Number 7 is ready…" Davies, *Ibid.*

13. "…After I am gone." Davies, page 111.

14. Subordinate rolled out Hobey's old Spad Number 2. Davies, page 106.

15. "…climbed into the cockpit." Herring, Donald, November 1, 1957 letter to *Princeton Alumni Weekly*.

16. "…promise once more that he would fly straight out…" Herring, *Ibid.*

17. "I started to run…" Herring, *Ibid.*

18. "…prayed it might happen." Herring, *Ibid.*

19. "…risk getting back on the field." Herring, *Ibid.*

20. "They are very heavy and lose height remarkably fast." Baker, Hobey, May 27, 1918 letter to father, Mudd Box 1, folder 2.

21. "Engine buried in the soft ground," Herring, 11/1/57, *PAW*.

22. "He died in my arms." Herring, Donald, February 5, 1959 letter to Andrew Turnbull, Mudd, Box 1, folder 2.

23. Singing of 'Nearer my God to Thee.' Frazier, George *Boston Herald* column, December, 1962.

24. Baker might have saved his life… *NYT,* January 23, 1919.

25. "I sat down to read..." Bauhan, Rolf, April 27, 1962 letter to George Frazier, Mudd Box 4.
26. "Baker Dies in Fall of Airplane" *NYT,* December 27, 1918.
27. "...having a celebration together." Bauhan letter, *Ibid.*
28. "...Fiancée Reported Married in Paris." Davies, page 113.
29. "If ever a man deliberately nosed down..." Gurnee, O.T., *Lexington Herald,* November 16, 1919.
30. "...a daring thief stole my briefcase from between my feet." Herring, Donald, November 1, 1957 Herring letter to *PAW.*

CHAPTER FOURTEEN: For the Love of Hobey

1. "The pride of Princeton." *NYT,* February 6, 1919.
2. "Divine disregard for his own safety." Davies, page 110.
3. Hobey Baker Memorial Rink donation statistics. Davies, page 112.
4. Deeded his one-half share of the farmhouse... Archer, J.P. Correspondence December 2017
5. Body of Hobey's anticipated arrival. Archer, *Ibid.*
6. Lone officer attending casket. *Philadelphia Evening Bulletin* July 15, 1921.
7. Total St. Paul's men who died in WWI. Saint Paul's School Archives, *The Roll of Honor: St. Paul's School and the Great War 1914-18.*
8. Hobey Eulogy: "A fine sample of American Manhood." *Philadelphia Enquirer,* July 20, 1921
9. Hobey's prominent headstone. Archer, Joseph Patrick, "Hobey's Anonymous Epitaph," manuscript, 2018 (reprinted as Afterword, infra).
10. A female writer whose pen name was "Amory Hare." Archer, Joseph Patrick, "Hobey Baker's Epitaph: Anonymous No Longer." *Princeton Alumni Weekly,* Nov. 3, 2016.
11. Mary Amory Hare's ode to cousin Hobey. *Princeton Alumni Weekly,* April 9, 1918.

CHAPTER FIFTEEN: Suicide? The Great Debate

1. "...Hobey's death was not entirely accidental." Fimrite, Ron, *Sports Illustrated,* "A Flame That Burned Too Brightly," March 18, 1991.

2. "The rumor of his suicide persists to this day…" Davies, p. 109.

3. "…this is the way he wanted to go." Fischler, Stan, interview, November, 2017.

4. "…maybe, maybe…." Hardy, Stephen interview, December 2017.

5. "…he wasn't going back to Wall Street." Smith, Bruce, interview, October 2017. In the early 1990's, Smith moved to the Rocky Mountains to pen the ultimate Hobey screenplay. It was sold and registered in Hollywood by the Kennedy Marshall agency. Smith's fascination with Hobey was not yet satisfied, so eh sculpted a bronze statue of the legend that today resides in the Hockey Hall of Fame in Toronto.

6. The Hollywood rumor mill generated a story that Leonardo DiCaprio considered one of two screenplays in 2003 for his next project: *Aviator* and *Hobey Baker*. DiCaprio chose the former, and Hobey returned to a dusty shelf. Smith then teamed up with Rick Sloane in 2017 to take another stab at getting Hobey onto the big screen, a "more romantic version."

7. "Nah, I don't think so." Lally, Paul, February, 2018 interview.

8. "Even a green pilot wouldn't have done that." Woolley, Charles, interview, Golden.

9. "…and I never knew any who would have committed suicide." Herring, Donald, February 6, 1959 letter to Henry Baker, Mudd, Box 1, folder 2.

10. "…no such comment would have any merit." Bauhan, Rolf, April 27, 1962 letter to George Frazier, Mudd Box 4.

11. "This from the mouths of pilots that saw him fall…" Cushman, Holbrook 1960 letter to John Davies, Mudd, Box 1, folder 2.

12. "…a crash is apt to come to anyone." Baker, Hobey, November 22, 1917 letter to father, Mudd, Box 1, folder 1.

13. "…avoid the embarrassment of a crash landing off the field." Archer, J.P., correspondence March, 2018.

14. "…a courageous gentleman like Hobey Baker." Biddle, Charles, June 24, 1966 letter to John Davies, Mudd, Box 1, folder 2.

E P I L O G U E : Parental Postscript

1. "…they may show up some day." Baker, Hobey, November 21, 1918 letter to father, Mudd, Box 1, folder 2.

2. Locomotor Ataxia. Alfred Baker Burial Form, Nassau Presbyterian Church, Princeton, N.J. Also on FindAGrave.com, citing death certificate.

3. "Invalid." Davies, page 50.

4. Symptoms of Tabes Dorsalis. MedicinePlus.Gov

5. "…missing…location of ashes unknown." FindAGrave.com

6. West Laurel Hill Cemetery Modus Operandi. Archer, Joseph Patrick. December, 2017 Correspondence.

INDEX

As a sports producer, TIM RAPPLEYE has covered eight Olympic Games, earning two Emmy Awards along the way. His last book, *Jack Parker's Wiseguys*, earned raves for its poignant story-telling from the heart of hockey's hub in Boston. Rappleye has been pursuing the Hobey Baker story for over two decades, and this book is the culmination of a professional lifetime of research and heady debate.

CPSIA information can be obtained
at www.ICGtesting.com
Printed in the USA
BVHW071342161218
535732BV00003BA/421/P